Prayer Works

Getting a Grip on
Catholic Spirituality

Matthew Leonard

Nihil Obstat
Msgr. Michael Heintz, Ph.D.
Censor Librorum

Imprimatur
✠ Kevin C. Rhoades
Bishop of Fort Wayne-South Bend
January 14, 2014

The *Nihil Obstat* and *Imprimatur* are official declarations that a book is free from doctrinal or moral error. It is not implied that those who have granted the *Nihil Obstat* and *Imprimatur* agree with the contents, opinions, or statements expressed.

Except where noted, the Scripture citations used in this work are taken from the *Catholic Edition of the Revised Standard Version of the Bible* (RSV), copyright © 1965 and 1966 by the National Council of the Churches of Christ in the United States of America. Used by permission. All rights reserved.

Excerpts from the *Catechism of the Catholic Church, Second Edition*, for use in the United States of America, copyright © 1994 and 1997, United States Catholic Conference — Libreria Editrice Vaticana. Used by permission. All rights reserved.

Every reasonable effort has been made to determine copyright holders of excerpted materials and to secure permissions as needed. If any copyrighted materials have been inadvertently used in this work without proper credit being given in one form or another, please notify Our Sunday Visitor in writing so that future printings of this work may be corrected accordingly.

ISBN 978-1-61278-780-0 (Inventory No. T1586)
eISBN: 978-1-61278-357-4
LCCN: 2014938932

Cover design: Patty Borgman
Cover artwork:Reni, Guido - St. James the Greater, Google Art Project
Interior design: Maggie Urgo

Printed in the United States of America

CONTENTS

Foreword

By Brant Pitre

I will never forget the day I first discovered the classic Catholic teaching on the three kinds of prayer—vocal prayer, meditation, and contemplation—and the three stages of spiritual growth—the purgative, illuminative, and unitive ways.

It happened one night while I was sorting through boxes of books that a priest friend had donated to me from his personal theological library. Several boxes were filled spiritual classics written by saints and mystics like St. Catherine of Siena, St. John of the Cross, St. Teresa of Avila, and St. Francis de Sales. They also contained modern books on spiritual theology.

One book in particular caught my eye because it had the words "perfection" and "contemplation" in the title—two things about which I knew absolutely nothing.

Don't get me wrong. As a Professor of Scripture, I was well aware that in the Sermon on the Mount, Jesus says to his disciples: "You, therefore, must be perfect, as your heavenly Father is perfect" (Matthew 5:48). But I had often wondered whether Jesus really meant it—at least as far I was concerned. For if I knew anything about myself, it was that I was very, very far from perfect.

Likewise, although I had heard of contemplative prayer, I had certainly never experienced anything remotely like what I imagined it to be. Growing up Catholic, my experience of prayer consisted primarily of saying the words of the Our Father, the Hail Mary, or the Glory Be. I assumed that contemplative prayer, whatever it might be, was not for a layman like myself.

Now, I don't recall anyone actually ever actually saying that contemplation wasn't for someone like me. However, somewhere along the way, I picked up the idea that while monks and nuns might be called to contemplative union with God, the best I could hope for as a layman living in the world was spiritual mediocrity and (hopefully) not going to hell.

Yet as I began to read, I discovered that the spiritual classics teach that *every single Christian* is called to true holiness. As the letter to the Hebrews says, all are called to "the holiness without which no one will see the Lord" (Hebrews 12:14). Moreover, I also stumbled on to the ancient Christian belief that, just as ordinary biological life goes through *three stages* of growth—childhood, adolescence, and adulthood—so too, the spiritual life ordinarily involves three stages of growth—purgation, illumination, and union with God.

These discoveries totally transformed the way I saw my own prayer life. Up to that point, I had always thought of my spiritual life as a kind of "revolving door." On one side of the door was mortal sin; on the other side, a state of grace. As I saw it, my main goal was to avoid dying on the wrong side of the door!

Yet here were the great Catholic mystics telling me that God had much, much more in store for me. Here were canonized saints teaching me that the spiritual life was not a revolving door, but a *process* of growth. Here were the doctors of the Church insisting that every believer is called, by virtue of his or her baptism, to a life of vocal prayer, meditation and contemplation. Here were the greatest spiritual writers of all time telling me that contemplative prayer was not just important, but—to use the words of Jesus to Martha—"the one thing necessary" (Luke 10:42).

The question now was: *Where do I begin?* How do I learn to meditate? How do I start making progress in my spiritual life? Can I really ever experience the gift of contemplative prayer? How do I grow in virtue?

If you're anything like me, when I first started taking my spiritual life seriously and trying to read the spiritual classics like the *Dark Night of the Soul* by St. John of the Cross or The *Interior Castle* by St. Teresa of Avila, I felt almost completely lost. I needed someone to introduce me to the basics of the spiritual life so that I could understand what the saints were talking about.

That's what Matthew Leonard's wonderful book does so beautifully. Matthew has read the spiritual classics, studied them deeply, and been teaching them for years. Even more, he has a unique gift for explaining complex ideas in clear, accessible, and practical language. Finally, to top it all off, Matthew writes with a great sense of humor. He will challenge you to grow spiritually and make you laugh all in one sentence.

So, if you've ever wondered—Does prayer really work? — and —How should I do it? —then I invite you to sit down and begin reading a book that will not only inform you but transform you, your prayer, and your spiritual life in Christ.

CHAPTER 1

Why Pray?

Prayer is huge. And by huge I mean deep, very deep, all the way around. There are a lot of ins, outs, ups, and sometimes even downs (on our part) when communicating with God. Even prayer's facets have facets. And it's vital — you simply cannot have a relationship with God if you're not willing to learn about, and engage in, prayer.

The beautiful thing is that Catholic tradition provides the framework that helps us move toward our essential encounter with God. And I'm not just talking about litanies or Memorares, good though they are. I'm talking about the whole shebang.

This book is designed to help you take your life of prayer to new heights, even if you're just beginning (in which case any height is new). It's not just about the why, but the how. It's about the different kinds of prayer. It's about the different stages of prayer. We'll even get into the stages of the spiritual life first developed in ancient times. You might never have heard of them — I only came across them after my conversion when I had been a Catholic for nearly a decade. All this material is very important because prayer, when it is truly understood, is spiritual dynamite in the hands of a Catholic.

Dogged Prayer

Don't let anyone ever tell you prayer doesn't work. I'm not saying it always works the way you'd like — even the Rolling Stones knew that you get what you need, not always what you want — but it does work. If it didn't, I wouldn't have a dog. It's not that I don't like dogs, but to me they're like boats — better to know someone who has one. So how did I come to acquire fifty-five pounds of drooling, shedding, furry energy named Sam? Prayer. Not mine, of course, my kids'.

While prayer is always powerful, in the hands of a child it's a deadly weapon. Forget about the woman in the Gospel of Luke who kept bugging the judge (see Lk 18), any parent knows that when children want something badly enough, they suddenly forget the meaning of words like "not now," "no," or even "never in a million years." You're talking, vocal chords are vibrating, sound waves quiver through the air, but they no longer penetrate. The requests from your progeny keep coming like phone calls from a collection agency with the wrong number.

Only the most resolute of parents can endure the onslaught of children convinced their request is just. It's unfair, if you ask me. After all, they don't have to work at being little children, which is what Christ admonishes us to be (see Mt 18:3). As such, their intentions tend to be more pure — or in my case, pure-bred.

For years I had withstood the constant requests for a canine. Indeed, few fathers had ever harbored such secret pride in their resolve. Pharaoh? Please! A softhearted weenie. Even he eventually let God's firstborn-son Israel escape. I was far superior — it was my second-born that brought me to my knees.

After a day trip to Amish country, where I had heroically denied their repeated, forlorn petitions for one of the "buy now" puppies we happened upon, an 8½-by-11-inch piece of paper appeared on my refrigerator. Written by my seven-year-old daughter, it was titled, "Prayer for the white dog and a pig." (Don't even ask about the pork. This story is strictly about the dog.) It continued: "Please, Jesus, help Dad know what I want the most and help him to understand how much I want the dog and pig. Help him to let us get the dog and the pig. Amen."

My laughter at the note simply covered the tremors that gently began to rattle my bones. I knew I was in some trouble. As the months went by the prayers continued, along with the interminable requests. One fateful day, when my patience had finally waned to the point of exasperation, I committed a grave error. "The only way we're going to get a dog," I forcefully declared, "is if God brings one right to us." There! It was over! Finality! I thought I had closed the door. In reality, it was the opening they needed.

Not long after I made my fateful declaration I was sitting outside with my two youngest children. From out of nowhere, in a neighborhood where I had never even seen a stray, a fine looking golden-haired dog came running down the street — alone. I glanced around. Not a human in sight. Mere seconds after pausing under a tree near us, the pooch was assaulted by the "love" of my two-year-old, who mauled him with affection. Shockingly, he never moved or showed the slightest agitation. I was impressed. When my daughter was finished, he moved on.

Curiously, the encounter stuck in my head that evening. "He sure handled Sophie's rough love well," mused the angel on my shoulder. "Not many dogs would."

"But she'll grow up, and he never will!" my dark side answered.

"This could be something God wants," responded the angel.

"Not a chance," came the scowling voice of reason. "He doesn't want to add to your workload."

To my chagrin, the dog remained on my mind, and the mental pinball continued the next day. "I can totally see God answering the prayers of my children," I thought. "A hound from heaven. That would be just like him."

"Forget it! You'll have to walk him when it's freezing outside. Every day!"

"On the other hand, if you reverse the letters of 'God' it spells ..."

Clearly I was in crisis. I couldn't shake it off. I was being haunted by a live dog. I knew it would please the kids immensely, but I also knew it would destroy the last shred of peace in my life (which was a figment of my imagination to begin with). Finally, I had a man-to-man with God, just to get things straight.

"I can't even believe I'm saying this at all, God, but if you want me to have this dog," I stated flatly, "he's going to have to come back." I thought this was pretty big of me, since I at least allowed for the slight possibility it could happen. Of course, in my favor were odds even Vegas would love. No way this stray comes back. Quieting my angst, I put on my shoes and headed outside with my kids.

Five minutes later the same dog, tongue hanging out sideways, made his way right to my driveway. Only this time, he was being walked on a leash by a man and woman. "Thank you, God!" I practically exclaimed. I was off the hook. God had heard the cry of my heart. I felt like singing, but I was never more wrong in my life. (Except for that time when I didn't think stapling my finger would hurt.)

To make a long story short, the couple walking the dog had picked him up off the street. We talked for thirty minutes about mutual friends, philosophy classes with my father-in-law (small world), and, of course, dogs — particularly the dog panting at my feet. They were planning on taking the pup to the pound the next day and said if I wanted him to let them know. I took their number, mostly to be polite, and let them go.

That's when the guilt set in. I tried to shut it out of my mind, but I had told God what I had told God. Cursing my colossal moment of insanity, I mentioned the encounter to my wife, who was totally siding with the kids on this issue. Smelling blood in the water, my children appeared out of nowhere like monsters from the deep. I knew it was over.

After a few vain, halfhearted attempts to snatch victory from the jaws of defeat — reminding them of the disgusting tasks required of dog owners while they unanimously, like children all over the world, countered that these weren't a problem — I set off after the couple on the first vehicle I could get my hands on, my daughter's pink bike. Tossing aside manhood like an empty lighter, I raced down the street in full view of my neighbors. It mattered little. My pride had been crushed under the weight of my children's prayers and my own rash pronouncements. Let them stare. I was on a mission from dog — I mean, God.

Naturally Religious

The goal of the spiritual life, and prayer in particular, is intimacy with God. Of course, that wasn't first and foremost on my children's minds when they began storming heaven for a puppy. Nevertheless, the fact that they began to pray in the first place says they understood at least some of the value and power of prayer. They knew where to turn in order to get something clearly beyond their own power to acquire. Everybody does.

Whether or not people realize it, this understanding of an "Other" outside of us to whom we can turn is inside everyone. It's not as if Christianity made up praying any more than it made up the notion of religion. Both have been a part of civilization from the beginning. Aztecs, Egyptians, Martians, it doesn't matter. Religion has been around as long as we have.

For some reason I'm amused when I hear references to a formerly bad person who "got religion" and is now a better person. A person doesn't "get" religion. You can't buy it on the

Web or find it at the store. You don't need to. Made in the image of God, every person is religious by nature. "The desire for God is written in the human heart" (CCC 27). Echoing the *Catechism of the Catholic Church*, Pope Benedict XVI said that deep inside we know there is "Another" outside of us to whom we owe homage, to whom we can turn. This built-in desire for God, says the pope, is the soul of prayer.[1]

Prayer expresses our thirst for God, and is as natural as speaking itself. When people first reach out to their Maker, for whatever reason, it's almost always in the form of a prayer: "God, if you're really there…" "God, if you can hear me…" "God, please help me!" We cry out to God when we are in need. The old adage "there are no atheists in foxholes" is usually true because in danger of death there is a deep awareness our lives are not solely our own. There is an "Other" who *must* be there to offer assistance.

Crises tend to bring this truth to the fore. Civilizations have advanced quite a bit over the last few hundred years, and many of us are pretty comfortable these days. But contrary to popular belief, the world and everyone in it cannot be saved by inventions or technical progress. (Have you ever heard anyone beg for his iPhone on his deathbed?) Can money save? Nope. Politics? *Puhleez!*

We need to get back to basics and rediscover the necessity of prayer. The flow of saving grace doesn't happen without it. "No one can be saved without God's help," says St. Augustine, and "no one asks His help but the one who prays."[2]

God's help through prayer isn't just a necessity for first-timers like those guys in foxholes, either. If you used to walk with God but no longer do, odds are it's because you stopped praying. "All who have been lost were lost because they did not pray," according to St. Alphonsus Liguori.[3] People stop praying for all kinds of reasons. And one of the main culprits, I think, is a misunderstanding of what it means to lead a spiritual life.

It's All Good

That misunderstanding stems from a very common belief that growth in prayer and the spiritual life is focused solely on denial of self: pain and suffering. We've got to beat ourselves into submission like those monks in *Monty Python and the Holy Grail* chanting *"Pie Iesu Domine"* ("Pious Lord Jesus") while continually cracking themselves in the head. And unless you're a bit strange, it's kind of hard to get excited about this process. After all, we want to enjoy life. We get only one turn on the merry-go-round, and it should be exciting and fun.

It's hard to find fault with this view of things. There's no denying the world God gave us is full of wonder and beauty, and like any good father, he wants us to enjoy it. But if this is the full extent of our outlook, we're missing the boat. It's a limited, shortsighted perspective that will undermine our spiritual life.

If we're stuck on this world — if we let our love of created things blind us to the reality of the Creator — then we can't raise our eyes to the next. Our natural vision must become supernatural because, as great as the universe is, it's only a foreshadowing of what is to come. When we renounce our search for fulfillment in *this* world, we give up something "good" for the inconceivable greatness of the *next* world.

Sometimes we hold back because it seems painful. And, yes, there can be a certain kind of discomfort involved in letting go of this world. But growth in the spiritual life isn't misery — it's ecstasy! We die to ourselves so as to live. Anything we suffer here on earth is so that "we may also be glorified with him," says St. Paul in Romans 8:17. But it's not just about a great afterlife. It's about an abundant, adventurous, fulfilling life now.

Prayer leads to an intimacy with the Person who made all the stuff of this world — and he did it simply by speaking. Imagine that. In a mere instant he created all the things at which we keep grasping for satisfaction. But God is offering us something far better. Something he's been preparing for all eternity: himself. He is the *more* we desire. He is the only *more* that can fill us up, and that filling starts right now through the sacraments, empowered by prayer.

Prayer helps us begin receiving the goodness of God. It lifts the veil of this world little by little, giving us glimpses of the glory to come. The more we pray, the more we understand we're living for him: a living, breathing relationship with God is the only thing that can ever fill us up.

It Is Well with My Soul

Remember the encounter between Jesus and the Samaritan woman at the well in the Gospel of John? Jesus asks the woman to draw water for him to drink. She's surprised because Jews didn't normally mix with Samaritans. Jesus responds to her surprise by saying, "If you knew the gift of God, and who it is that is saying to you, 'Give me a drink,' you would have asked him and he would have given you living water" (4:10).

Being a practical woman, she points out that he doesn't even have a jar, so how is he going to get her some of this "living water." Then Jesus delivers the kicker:

> Every one who drinks of this water will thirst again, but whoever drinks of the water that I shall give him will never thirst; the water that I shall give him will become in him a spring of water welling up to eternal life. (4:13-14)

Jesus knows our longings. He knows we're thirsty. And he knows he can quench that thirst. That's why he offers himself to us and is constantly seeking us out. All we have to do is accept him. That's where prayer comes in. It's "the encounter of God's thirst with ours" (CCC 2560).

And note it's not just for later. We're not just talking about heaven. The "living water" he offers begins to fill us up now, slaking our present thirst and "welling up to eternal life" until we are perfected.

Prayer is vitally important because we are called by Christ to "be perfect, as your heavenly Father is perfect" (Mt 5:48). But perfection isn't a thing, so to speak, it's a person — God. Personal perfection, therefore, is not the be-all and end-all. Not even the greatest ethical behavior is enough to make a person a saint. God is perfect, and prayer makes us more like God, and that's why prayer is important (see CCC 2572).

Prayer, in fact, is one of the most amazing gifts ever. You wouldn't dream of being able to pick up the phone and immediately reach the CEO of Apple, IBM, or some other multinational corporation, would you? You'd be hard-pressed to get the owner of your local grocery store on the line, for crying out loud. But the God of the universe makes himself constantly at our disposal. Like a Blondie disk on constant repeat, our Father is saying, "Call me! (call me) Call me anytime."

Of course, there's a whole lot of technology that goes into even the simplest phone call. Similarly, there's "spiritual technology" that goes into any conversation with the Almighty. And the more we understand what prayer is and how to do it, not even the sky is the limit of our spiritual progress.

As we move forward in this book, I want you to keep one point in mind: Our goal, as the spiritual master Fr. Eugene Boylan wrote, is "to get in touch with Jesus as early as possible in the spiritual life, in each of its exercises, especially that of prayer, and to keep in touch with Him by all possible means and at all costs."[4]

CHAPTER 2

What Is Prayer?

You can't get to know people without talking with them. This is true in every relationship (except for mimes). For example, I didn't ask my wife to marry me when I first met her. I waited a good three hours. Okay, maybe I didn't actually ask her out loud, but I started thinking about my proposal pretty quickly after our first encounter. Even so, I knew I needed to get to know her. More important, I knew she needed to get to know me before being willing to go on a date with me, much less say, "I do." So we started to talk. I called her. I called her. I called her ... (pause for effect) ... then finally she called me. Whew!

When we first met, I was living in Chicago and she was in eastern Ohio. Being so far apart, we spoke on the phone a lot and e-mailed constantly. The distance was challenging, but we were thankful we could communicate through modern means. (For our tenth anniversary I had our many e-mails bound in a book titled "From E-male to Female.") With all that conversation we actually started to get to know each other. In spite of that, she actually said "yes" to my proposal the following year, and we're approaching our thirteenth anniversary as I write.

As a man proposes to the love of his life, in a similar way God proposes to us. That's what's been happening from the beginning of time. In fact, that's what the Bible is all about. It's a story of God's love for humanity that culminates with "the marriage supper of the Lamb" (Rv 19:9).

Aside from people who celebrate their vows at the Elvis Chapel in Vegas, this relationship unfolds through conversation. And our conversation with God is prayer. It's how we fall in love with him and how God starts to reveal himself to us, akin to the way Veronica and I began to reveal ourselves to each other in all those phone calls and e-mails.

But it's more than that. As we converse with God, he's slowly conforming us to himself. As noted in the last chapter, he's making us like him.

Have you ever noticed that people pick up the speech patterns, ideas, and habits of the people they hang out with? For instance, one day your kid comes home and drops a "colorful" word that you would never use (except at the bowling alley). A parent's immediate response is practically universal: "Where did you learn that?" (We never assume it was from us.) It's natural for people to start to sound like those around them. I spent the first six years of my life in Texas, and whenever I speak at a conference or parish in the South and hear the word "y'all," it's not long before I'm "y'alling" all over the place. It's incredible. In mere moments my mind decides the phrase "all of you" is too tiring and cumbersome and I slip back into my native tongue. (I even start craving grits and fried okra.)

It's the same in our relationship with God. We were born to be part of his family. Sin disrupted our relationship, but the more time we spend together, the more we become like him again. We start to talk like him, think like him, and even act like him. We're getting back to our roots. In fact, the *Catechism* says that "prayer restores man to God's likeness" (2572). It's a divine gift.

Often, we make the mistake of viewing prayer in terms of something we have to do. That's not totally wrong, because we do have to make an act of the will and follow through. But prayer isn't primarily something we do for God. It's something he does for us. It starts with him. It is his thirst for us that drives the relationship. In prayer, God is planting and watering seeds of love in our hearts. Everything he does centers on self-gift, and prayer is no exception. He wants us to pray, to turn toward him, person to person, so he can give himself to us.

And we shouldn't be afraid he won't like what he'll find. God already knows us inside, outside, upside down. (Love that book.) It's not as if after the conversation gets started he's going to suddenly exclaim, "Well, I never knew you did that!" or "I can't believe you think those thoughts!" He made us. He knows us more than we know ourselves.

Rather than revealing us to God, prayer reveals God to us. And the more we see and understand, the more we love. We begin to recognize who he is and to praise him. But in order to understand what prayer is and how it works, we must first understand who we are and what we are created to be — namely, God's children.

Sometimes I cringe when I say "God's children," because the image that comes to mind is one of those kitschy pictures with a kindly Jesus sitting in a nice, grassy space with little kids seated around him. (It's always vexed me that he's invariably in biblical-era robes and the children are dressed in pants, overalls, and dresses.) That image has value for Sunday school and children's Bibles, but I think it has potential to damage a true understanding of our identity as members of God's family. It's a bit banal, not to mention unrealistic (those kids would be climbing all over him). So let's dig into what it means to be a real child of God.

Family First

God is our Father. But he's not just ours. He's also Father in relation to the other members of the Trinity: the Son and the Holy Spirit. His Fatherhood isn't an analogy, either. It's who he is. This fact — one of the deepest truths of our faith — tells us something vitally important — namely, that God is family. He's not like a family, he is family. St. John Paul II said that "God in his deepest mystery is not a solitude, but a family because he has within himself Fatherhood, Sonship, and the essence of the family which is love."[5]

Father, Son, and Holy Spirit form the family of God, and you and I are members of this family, created to be part of this family. In other words, salvation history, the story of how we are saved, is family history.

This is evident throughout Scripture. Our first parent, Adam, was created to be a "son of God" (Lk 3:38). God the Father is also the origin of the whole "get out of your parent's house and find a wife" thing — that is, leave and cleave (see Gn 2:24). And it continues from there. The Israelites are God's firstborn son (Ex 4:22); Solomon is God's own son (2 Sm 7:14); honoring father and mother is even part of the Ten Commandments (Ex 20:12). And don't even consider forgetting all those "this guy begat that guy" and "that guy begat this guy" stuff, which terrifies countless lectors.

The reason you see family language in Scripture, indeed the reason human society is based on families, is because God is family. He created us to live this way. St. Paul says, "For this reason I bow my knees before the Father, from whom every family in heaven and on earth is named" (Eph 3:14-15).

So the Bible is essentially the story of how God created us to be in his family and how he worked to get humanity back into that family after Adam got us kicked out. That story, of course, culminates in Jesus Christ. And this is where the story changes — a lot.

Adam and Solomon and others might have been called "son of God," but only Jesus is *the* "Son of God" (Lk 1:35, Jn 20:31, Rom 1:4). And his identity as such ushers in a whole new way of praying. Unlike those who preceded him in history, his is true filial prayer — the prayer of Son to Father. It's the prayer of family. It's the kind of prayer "which the Father awaits from his children ... lived out by the only Son in his humanity, with and for men" (CCC 2599). In other words, our prayer is in the Son, Jesus Christ.

As we saw in the first chapter, people have been praying since there have been people. "Prayer is bound up with human history, for it is the relationship with God in historical events," says the *Catechism* (see 2568). All the main characters in Scripture — Abraham, Moses, David, Elijah, Mary, and so many others (even bad guys) — were praying. But Jesus has a unique identity.

The Second Person of the Trinity became human like the rest of us (except for sin, says Hebrews 4:15) so that he could represent all of humanity back to the Father. He wedded a perfect human nature to his divine nature, joining them forever. Because he is all God and all man at the same time, he can represent both sides of the equation. He's playing both sides, so to speak. He represents God to us and us to God. And this is the key to prayer. We can pray to God *like* Christ because we are *in* Christ.

Starting with our baptism, we are incorporated into the Mystical Body of Christ and become "sons in the Son," joined to him in a real way. When we say we're children of God, therefore, we're not simply using a figure of speech. We have been transformed through a divine adoption and gained a new identity. God is our Father, and Jesus is our brother. Through the grace wrought by Christ, we begin a process of becoming more and more like him until we are fully and finally united with him in heaven.

This is big news, because it's a big change.

Before the time of Jesus, people could interact with God on friendly terms, for sure. Exodus 33:11 says Moses used to speak "face to face" with God, "as a man speaks to his friend." They were buddies. But Christ brought the relationship to a whole new level. As the Son of God, he cries out to the Father and actually calls him "Abba, Father" (Mk 14:36). And in him, we can do the same. St. Paul declares that we have received a "spirit of sonship," so that "when we cry 'Abba!' Father! it is the Spirit himself bearing witness with our spirit that we are children of God" (Rom 8:15-16). This is our new reality in the New Covenant of Jesus Christ.

And from the moment of his conception, Christ's life is a perfect prayer, a perfect offering to the Father. Through prayer, through the sacraments he offers and extends this same life to us. The deeper our union with Christ, the more perfect our life of prayer becomes. Christ is our prayer power source.

Jesus made a new identity and new mode of prayer available to us, but he practiced the art of prayer as a man of his times, learning all the different forms and types of prayers that the other Jews learned. It's the same with us. Catholic prayer comes in all kinds of shapes and sizes, such as blessing and adoration, prayers of petition, intercession, thanksgiving, and praise. Each of these puts a little different spin on our interaction with God. For example, the prayer of blessing is in response to God's gifts. In petition, we're making our needs known. Through the prayer of adoration we exalt "the greatness of the Lord" and recognize God's kingship (see CCC 2628).

We'll touch on some of the other forms of prayer mentioned above as we continue to move through our study on prayer. For now, let's talk about the two most basic types of prayer in which all those previous forms of prayer fit. Following the lead of the great spiritual master Archabbot Benedict Baur, we'll call these two types "finite prayer" and "constant prayer."[6]

Finite Prayer

What is it that makes a prayer prayer? Is it thinking really hard about what you're saying? Is it being able to conjure up the right image of Our Lady when you're praying a Rosary? (She looks best in blue, of course.) How about the warm fuzzies — that nice little burst of emotion we sometimes get? Is that prayer? Nope. None of those things are bad — in fact, they're good — but prayer can exist without any of them.

Quoting St. Thérèse of Lisieux, the *Catechism* calls prayer a "surge of the heart" (2558). The last Father of the Church, St. John Damascene, says it "is the raising of one's mind and heart to God or the requesting of good things from God" (CCC 2559). Finite prayer is an active form of prayer in which we're consciously making an effort to seek God. We're raising our hearts and minds to God through blessing, adoration, petition, thanksgiving, praise, and so forth. Finite prayer stops and starts as we determine.

In its essence, all prayer is an act of love. That's why God never tires of our prayers, just as your beloved never tires of the sweet nothings you whisper in his or her ear. In prayer we're whispering our love to a God who *is* love (see 1 Jn 4:8). We stop looking inward and turn our gaze toward our true Beloved.

No longer thinking so much about ourselves, we start thinking more about him. In fact, it's not hard to figure out whether or not we're growing in prayer (and it has nothing to do with feelings). If we're not turning more and more away from the world and becoming more and more like Jesus Christ, there's something wrong. Prayer is meant to restore us to the likeness of God and in so doing give him glory.

We begin that process by engaging in particular types of finite, active prayer. But it's only the beginning.

Constant Prayer

Finite, active prayer is meant to lead us to habitual, or constant, prayer. That's the name of the game, the golden goose of the spiritual life. Quoting the ancient monk Evagrius Ponticus, the *Catechism* states, "We have not been commanded to work, to keep watch and to fast constantly, but it has been laid down that we are to pray without ceasing" (2742). Of course, we're all familiar with St. Paul's admonition to "pray constantly." As a kid I remember thinking: "Seriously, Paul? Not only are people going to think I'm nuts as I walk around muttering to myself, but multi-tasking is not natural to my gender." But before we knock Paul off his high horse (again), let's take a moment to see what he means.

Constant prayer is not an act of prayer, so to speak. Otherwise we wouldn't be able to perform our duties in life. (Forget about texting, I've nearly wrecked my car on several occasions while attempting the Rosary on the freeway.) So what is Paul talking about? He's referring to a permanent attitude, one rooted in trustful surrender and merging of our will to God's. It's an inner peace that accepts whatever happens as God's good will for our life. It doesn't mean we just sit back and do nothing, but rather that we have an attitude of cheerful compliance founded on the knowledge that what God wants us to experience is best.

Constant prayer is fed by acts of finite prayer which operate on the "surface" of the soul. We makes acts of the will that move us into closer union with God and cause the embers of love in our hearts to glow more fiercely even when we're not engaged in active, finite prayer.

Of course, the reverse is also true. Constant prayer feeds and fuels our acts of prayer so they become more focused and fruitful. And when we can establish a state of constant prayer, submitting ourselves gladly to God's will, everything we do becomes an act of prayer.

A Little Privacy, Please!

Since we're all members of the same Body of Christ, prayer has both a personal and communal dimension. That being said, it's primarily between you and God. Even when you're praying with a group of people, such as at Mass, prayer has a personal character. You are lifting your voice to God along with others. It's a private conversation between hearts in the context of family worship.

The beauty of communal prayer is that it shows the unity of the body of believers, God's family, something he certainly desires. But let's be honest, not all conversation is meant for public consumption. I don't really care to know the intimate details or secrets of Joe Catholic next to me, nor do I want to share mine with him. Sharing is not always caring.

Prayer is primarily personal because, ultimately, I can't rely upon other people to establish my relationship with God. I can't hide behind the crowd. Each of us is going to stand in front of God at the end of our life, and the depth of our relationship will be fully exposed at that moment. We won't be thinking about the person in front of or behind us in line. It'll be just each of us and God.

That's why it's so crazy not to pray. Yet even when we know it's good for us, we're good at inventing lame excuses. We're too tired. We've got too much work to do. We need to organize our sock drawer. The list goes on and on and on. Look, I get it. I'm in the same boat. It's not easy. We're dealing with weaknesses that have plagued humanity since Adam and Eve exercised some very poor decision-making skills back in the garden.

Nevertheless, there are no real excuses. God gives us every grace we need to pray. More than that, think about what we're avoiding — life in God! We're actually looking for a way out of the only family on earth that doesn't need counseling. We're shunning the offer of a lifetime. We're trying to get out of eternal bliss! So let's stop the insanity and start to dive even deeper into prayer.

CHAPTER 3

Prayer and the Purgative Way

In the first chapter we noted that Christ calls us to be perfect, and we looked at the role of prayer in making that happen. We also discussed how personal perfection isn't the end, so to speak. That's the final outcome, but the whole point of the spiritual life, including our prayer life, is to become like God. Becoming like God means becoming perfect.

But how exactly does that happen? How does something become perfect? Sounds a bit difficult, doesn't it?

St. Thomas Aquinas tells us there is a sense in which perfection happens when something finally achieves what it was created for. A seed is perfected when it becomes a tree, for example. A tadpole finds its end when it becomes a frog. A pig eventually becomes bacon. That is its created end. It has achieved its delicious destiny.

It's the same with us. We are perfected when we finally grow into what we were made to be — "partakers of the divine nature" (2 Pt 1:4). "Did you say 'divine,' Matt?" Yes, but don't misunderstand. We don't become all powerful, all knowing, or present everywhere like God, because we always remain creatures. But through God's grace we become what he is by nature. It's a gift. We become true sons and daughters in the divine family of God. Created for union with God, we can't be perfect until we achieve that union with him.

So life essentially boils down to a journey to God. We're going to meet him one way or the other. It's either going to be a good meeting where he welcomes us into his presence, or it'll be a bad meeting where we are cast out because we rejected him by the way we lived our lives.

And if we're supposed to journey to God, that means there must be a definite road to travel. But we've got to find it. We need a map. A spiritual GPS. Otherwise, we're left driving in spiritual circles and the little voice in our head keeps repeating the word "recalculating."

The good news is Catholic doctrine and tradition provide that map, and it shows definite stages of the journey along a specific path. And I'm not just talking about going to Mass and confession and trying to pray. They are the vehicle, but they travel a particular path. And when we're in the right vehicle traveling the right path, we'll experience a transformation that leads to perfection.

The Science of Sainthood

This transformation is what some spiritual writers call "the science of sainthood." It's the movement of each person toward God that unfolds in distinct stages — we move along these stages in order to achieve union with God, to reacquire his likeness we lost through sin.

Just as maps come in different shapes and sizes and colors, there are many different spiritualities and charisms in the Catholic faith. It's one of the amazing features of our Church. We can't hope to cover all the different descriptions and methods associated with the "science of sainthood," so we're going to focus on the more traditional definitions of how this happens and what it looks like. The backbone of our discussion will be what many spiritual writers call the "Three Stages" or "Three Ages" of the spiritual life. They are the Purgative, Illuminative, and Unitive Ways.

Some of you are encountering these terms for the first time and you're thinking, "The Whoative and the Whatative?

I've been Catholic since before I was conceived, but I've never heard of this stuff."

Don't start trippin' on me. These are simply the classic stages of the spiritual life taught by the great masters of Catholic spirituality and prayer like Dionysius the Areopagite, Thomas Aquinas, John of the Cross, and many others.

The stages can be summarized like this: our lives need to be purged of sin — particularly mortal, or serious, sin — and vice. This is the Purgative Way, the beginning. We are then "illuminated" by the light and love of God in the second way, called the Illuminative Way. And we continue to be illuminated to the point where we are eventually unified with him in the final stage of spiritual growth — the Unitive Way.

St. Thomas Aquinas illustrates these stages in more human terms. He says we grow from spiritual childhood into adolescents, and finally into mature spiritual adulthood. These stages are sometimes also described as the way of beginners, proficients, and the perfect.

Knowledge of these stages is vitally important because they give us an understanding of where we are in the spiritual life. It's like one of those "You are here" maps. We need this because if we don't know where we are, we can't get to where we're going. So let's chat about the first part of the map, the initial stage, the Purgative Way.

The Purgative Way

About right now, you may be thinking: "The Purgative Way … well that doesn't sound so fun, Matt. In fact, it sounds like something along the lines of a colon cleanse." That's not too far off base. The Purgative Way involves a spiritual cleansing. It makes perfect sense when you think about it. After all, you can't get healthy until you've been purged of the diseases that are bringing you down.

But instead of looking at the negative side, let's look at the positive. What is really happening in the Purgative Way is the conversion of a soul from death to life. It's where we are born anew! Now that's pretty positive in my mind. The Purgative Way is the beginning of salvation because this is where a person moves from being in a state of mortal sin into a state of grace. We're not even close to perfect, but we're moving in the right direction.

A person enters the Purgative Way in one of two ways; either at baptism or, once they've lost their baptismal innocence, through confession. These sacraments are designed by God to get us into, or restore us to, the life of grace. If we are not in a state of grace, we are not in the Purgative Way. It assumes we are right with God through the sacraments.

Again, this initial stage of the spiritual life is like childhood. The spiritual child is constantly growing and learning. Not just about God, but about themselves, too. Just as babies gradually become aware of their hands and toes, spiritual children begin to recognize their faults as their spiritual poverty begins to make itself known. Their increasing knowledge of God instills a holy fear that helps keep them out of mortal sin.

I love the way St. Teresa of Ávila describes beginners in the spiritual life. Her description of how we move toward God in this life makes it easy to visualize the process.

St. Teresa was a Spanish mystic and is a Doctor of the Church — one of the great spiritual masters in the history of the Church. In her most famous work, *The Interior Castle*, she eloquently describes growth toward perfection using the imagery of a castle.

Teresa had a vision from Our Lord in which she saw the human soul as a crystal globe filled with seven different rooms or "mansions." These mansions were not arranged in the way you might expect, in a line, but rather, "some above, others below, others at each side; and in the center and midst of them all is the chiefest mansion where the most secret things pass between God and the soul."[7]

Each of the mansions was successively brighter, all of them illuminated by the King of Glory, who resided in the center of the globe in the seventh mansion. Outside the castle she described a great blackness infested by terribly foul and awful creatures like "toads, vipers, and venomous creatures."[8] These creatures represented sin and were the dark world a soul escapes when it begins a life of grace joined to Christ.

But in Teresa's description, a soul can be in a state of grace, in the Purgative Way, and still have not entered the castle. In other words, everyone has a castle, but not everyone goes in. These souls who don't, she says, are hanging around outside with the guards (no doubt smoking). And when they do finally enter, they allow in with them many of the poisonous beasties that were previously lurking outside.

How do you get into the castle? Teresa says a soul enters through prayer, particularly meditation (which we'll discuss in detail later). Prayer is huge for Teresa and all the spiritual writers. You can't overestimate its importance. She says souls without prayer are like paralytics. They have arms and legs, but can't control them.

Teresa wrote *The Interior Castle* in the first place because she was asked to write a treatise on prayer. And prayer is the main focus and topic of the last three mansions because she knew that spiritual growth and prayer cannot be separated.

So how does Teresa describe those in the early stages of the spiritual life? She says that souls who do eventually enter the first mansions are still overly concerned and consumed with the world. Even so, their desires are good. They want to grow. These souls will sometimes think about making some progress and will even pray a few times in a month. They're still battling with the poisonous snakes and vipers that slipped in with them, but they're on the right path.

Being so new to the spiritual life, though, these souls can easily make spiritually fatal choices. St. Teresa makes a point to emphasize how destructive and awful mortal sin is to the soul. While it never loses its splendor because it is created in the image of God, a soul in mortal sin can produce nothing but misery and filth. It is caked in grime. The brilliant light in the center of the soul is still there because God is always present, but his splendor is shrouded in darkness. Teresa stresses the awful nature of mortal sin because she wants to instill in us the fear of ever offending God. "O souls redeemed by the blood of Jesus Christ! ... Remove the pitch which blackens the crystal."[9]

Mortal sin is still a very real danger in the early mansions of *The Interior Castle* because the devil, says Teresa, has legions of fallen angels doing their best to deceive us and prevent us from passing on to the next mansions. Remember, the devil is the most envious of creatures. Envy isn't just jealousy. It's worse. Envy doesn't just want what the other person has. It wants to deprive the other person of what he has. The devil does not want you to have life. He wants to kill you. (If that doesn't shake you a bit, you need to read it again.)

This is very serious business. Satan and his demons will do whatever possible to prevent you from progressing in the spiritual life and attaining union with God because they hate you. "Be sober, be watchful. Your adversary the devil prowls around like a roaring lion, seeking some one to devour" (1 Pt 5:8).

Cleaning Up

What else can we say about people in the initial mansions or the Purgative Way? As they progress, they eventually begin to seriously focus on giving themselves to God. They attempt to avoid sin and to fight against the disordered desires of their heart which keep them from truly loving God: no more trashy television; they take a hard look at the music they listen to, the books and websites they read, all the things with which they fill their mind. They even try to keep quiet and not listen when friends are gossiping even though they really, really want to know what happened to so-and-so.

If beginners are truly seeking after the Lord, they eventually won't even try to excuse themselves when one of their faults comes into focus — and they will. God will show you how wretched and sinful you are, and it's a humbling experience. This process never really stops because the more you grow in the spiritual life the more you understand the depth of your sin. This is seen clearly in the life of St. Paul.

Early in his writings (see 1 Cor 15:9), Paul describes himself as "the least of the apostles." (Not bad, Paul. Nobody likes a bragger.) Later, in Ephesians, he says he is "the very least of all the saints" (3:8). (Nice. A little humility goes a long way.) Finally, near the end of years and years of unflinching devotion and service to the Lord, he declares he is the "chief" of sinners (1 Tm 1:15, King James Version). (Let's not get carried away here! You're St. Paul, after all!)

Notice he doesn't say, "I *was* the chief of sinners." After giving everything he had, truly loving the Lord by making a gift of his life, Paul says he *is* the chief of sinners. His relationship with God had grown so deep he came to a more full knowledge of the gulf between himself and God, a gulf that is overcome only by God's mercy.

This is an important point. The Lord reveals our sinfulness not so we'll be depressed, but so we'll run to him who is love and forgiveness. So when we notice our faults we want to correct them, not excuse them. Unfortunately, beginners in the spiritual life are famous for taking their eyes off themselves and noticing the faults of others: "Did you see the dress she was wearing last night? It was a bit short, wasn't it?"

"Uh huh ... I saw 'so and so' drinking what must have been his second beer, and it wasn't even the end of the first quarter!"

Jesus has very clear words for those of us who engage in these antics: "Judge not, that you be not judged. ... Why do you see the speck that is in your brother's eye, but do not notice the log that is in your own eye?" (Mt 7:1-3).

The Gain of Pain

Of course, one of the things we can't avoid talking about when discussing the stages of spiritual development is suffering. (Uh-oh.) On one hand, people serious about growing closer to God know they are going to have to deal with suffering. Everyone — Catholic, pagan, or just plain hedonist — has to deal with suffering in some way, shape, or form. No one can escape it.

It's like that classic scene in the movie *The Last of the Mohicans* where Daniel Day Lewis screams to Madeline Stowe before jumping through the waterfall, "I will find you!" Nobody escapes suffering. Adam's sin back in the Garden of Eden introduced suffering into this world, and now it's a part of all of our lives. Suffering always finds you — like an insurance salesman. The big difference between Catholics and everyone else is how we view it and deal with it. I don't have time to get into a long discussion of suffering, but we have to recognize it plays a vital role in the Purgative Way, as well as the rest of the spiritual life.

Ironically, we shudder at the thought of suffering in general terms, but many of us are more than willing to endure it for specific reasons, such as rippling abs and toned legs. Having spent a fair bit of time in my youth in weight rooms, I often heard my fellow gym rats screaming at each other what can only be described as motivation to suffer: "Feel the burn!" "Make it hurt!" "If you're not sore, you're not growing!" These "encouragements" — often accompanied by large amounts of spittle — were generally welcomed by the person exercising. They knew it was true. They knew they had to embrace the suffering so as to grow. ("Get big or get out!")

It's the same in the spiritual life. Just as we give up certain foods and force ourselves to exercise for our physical well-being, we need to wean ourselves from bad spiritual food and work out our spiritual muscles for our eternal well-being.

It's amazing, but Christ takes suffering and makes it the path to salvation. When we suffer, involuntarily or voluntarily through penance, and offer it to God, we become like Christ, who suffered and died for us so we could be saved. Yes, we're going to suffer one way or the other, but as Catholics we can make a simple act of the will — "Jesus, I give this suffering to you" — and it becomes a potent force for good. It can also lead to some powerful personal experiences.

Consolations

In return for this suffering and striving, many beginners in the spiritual life have discovered that God often rewards these generous souls with what we call "spiritual consolations" — tastes of heaven, sensible pleasures from above, even as they begin turning away from the sensible pleasures of this world.

Most often, these pleasures happen while you're praying. You might feel a tremendous peace or the presence of God in a way you've never experienced. You may feel overwhelmed with gratitude at how much God loves you, overcome by sheer delight and wonder as you seek him. You might even have a sensation of burning love for God that is palpable.

Even so, there is a danger in putting too much emphasis on these spiritual consolations. They might feel really good, but they are not the end goal, a mistaken notion held by many.

Before I became Catholic, I knew a guy who sold everything he had, packed his remaining belongings and family into a station wagon, and traveled from spiritual conference to spiritual conference trying to constantly experience manifestations of God. (He was like a spiritual "Dead Head.") But it doesn't work that way. These consolations are given by our

Father as an encouragement, a piece of spiritual candy that is a mere taste of what is to come. They're not the main course.

Hey, God! Where'd You Go?

So that we don't fall into the trap of focusing on these spiritual consolations, God brings us through what spiritual writers refer to as a second conversion. After we have traveled the length of the first stage, the Purgative Way, we come to a transition. St. John of the Cross calls it the "passive purification of the senses." Instead of spiritual delights, we begin to experience spiritual dryness. Prayer starts to be a little more difficult, and we just don't feel the presence of God the way we had. We're often left wondering — "Hey, God, where'd you go?"

What's happening is that we're being prepared to move into the second age of the spiritual life. We're starting to grow up. God is teaching us to seek after him for his own sake instead of just the sensible pleasure and spiritual candy with which we had associated him.

This second conversion begins to rid us of self-love. Why is this necessary? Because although we're growing, we're still immature. We still have trouble looking past our own needs. The world still revolves around us. Yes, we're developing a fervent love of God, but we still love ourselves more. So God seeks to purify us of this self-love by taking away some of the sensible pleasures he had previously given. Everything starts to get harder, like when school stopped being about coloring and snack time and became about homework.

In the second conversion, God is intensifying what he started in our first conversion, when we began the spiritual life. He's uprooting deeper weeds of sin. This stage is akin to junior high and early high school. We're on the cusp of adulthood. Our spiritual voice is changing. Our spiritual body is developing. We still do dumb stuff, but we're starting to mature.

Grow Up!

Now, at this point, a lot of people stop. They refuse to grow up spiritually. You know people like this in the natural world — perpetual children who never assume the responsibilities of adulthood. It's the same in the spiritual life when people choose to stop maturing and never become fully functioning spiritual adults.

And if for some reason you're thinking: "C'mon, Matt! Being an adult isn't always cupcakes and brownies. Sometimes I wouldn't mind being a kid again." Really? Would you rather go back to junior high? Need I remind you of puberty? Awkward dances? Figuring out how to unlock the padlock on your locker before the bell rings so you don't get detention along with a bunch of kids sporting Black Sabbath T-shirts and leather bracelets? And those were the girls! No thanks.

We undergo a second conversion to help us grow up. And just as in our natural lives, it's not altogether easy. St. John of the Cross compares it to a mother weaning her child, which can be mildly traumatic for all involved.[10] The most important thing to remember at this stage is to never stop, no matter what. We must be determined to seek after God at any cost, no matter what we feel or don't feel. And if we persevere through this purification, our senses submit more and more to the Spirit, and we gradually move out of the beginner stage into adolescence — the Illuminative Way. Phew!

CHAPTER 4

Illumination and Union

The Illuminative Way

The second stage of the spiritual life is all about falling in love. You start to love God not for what he does, but for who he is. And as you focus more on God, you begin to lose interest in the things of this world. I don't mean you don't care. Rather, you don't desire the things of this world as you did when you first embarked upon your journey to God.

You've probably experienced what I'm talking about on some level. Things become recognized for what they are — things. They can't satisfy you. That beautiful dress is merely a piece of fabric. That sweet car is simply a piece of metal that moves you from place to place. Your dream house simply doesn't excite anymore. You've lost your taste for this world and start to detach from it.

Some of you are whispering in your mind: "I don't *want* to lose my taste for this world. I have to live in it and I want to enjoy it." And I don't disagree with you. Life is meant for living to the full, something that Catholicism understands. Catholics view the world as good — ours is a very tactile religion, as we see in the sacraments and in our worship of God. We approach God through this physical world, and he wants us to enjoy this life.

But while he gave us this amazing universe and everything in it, we know at the end of the day it doesn't satisfy. This realization becomes stronger as you progress into the higher stages of the spiritual life and begin to long for the world to come. "No eye has seen, nor ear heard, nor the heart of man conceived what God has prepared for those who love him" (1 Cor 2:9).

Like previews of an upcoming blockbuster film, this world is just a foretaste of the glory ahead. As we mature and our gaze centers more on God, contemplating his wonders in prayer solidifies our identification with Paul, who declared, "For to me to live is Christ, and to die is gain" (Phil 1:21).

Sin in the Illuminative Way

Detachment from this world also helps us to love others more. We put others' needs in front of our own because we begin to love as Christ does. Interestingly, this love comes into play even when we sin. Unfortunately, we know sin can occur all the way up to the moment we die. In fact, an Irish priest once told me I'd stop sinning three days after I was dead. (He wasn't an optimist.) The difference is that once you hit this stage of the spiritual life sin isn't typically premeditated.

At this point a person is making a very conscious effort to grow in holiness. That means the kinds of sin he commits are different from what he used to commit. They're typically venial — that is, they don't totally destroy our relationship with God — and deal more with deeper issues like pride, lack of patience, vanity, and such.

Of course, it's still possible for a person in the Illuminative Way to fall into grave sin. But when that happens, what usually follows is a very contrite admission of guilt — we understand the value of what's been lost. We're quicker to repent and do so more deeply. Remember how bitterly St. Peter wept when he denied Our Lord?

Like Peter's, our sorrow is greater because we now understand our relationship to God as true sons and daughters. We're not servants fearing punishment. Rather, it kills us to know we've let our Father down. It's awful. Remember how bad it was when you expected your parents to spank you and instead they said, "I'm really disappointed in you." That was the worst!

And just as we don't go back to being children even when we do something childish, we don't start back at the beginning of the spiritual life even when we sin gravely. The only way we lose all of our progress is if we just chuck it all and go back to a life of spiritual death.

Don't Drink the Kool-Aid

Growth at this point is so powerful that, as crazy as it sounds, people in the higher stages of the spiritual life actually begin to embrace trials and suffering. Yup. You heard me right. Now a bunch of us who thought we were doing really well are thinking — "Guess I'm not quite as holy as I thought" or "Not sure I want to be that holy." Embrace suffering? Are you nuts? How can this possibly be? Well, it's kind of like Kool-Aid.

Remember when you were a kid and the promise of Kool-Aid left you jittery with excitement? You thought, "Wouldn't it be awesome if I could yell, 'Hey Kool-Aid!' and a giant red pitcher in a leotard would come crashing through the wall and pour me a delicious glass of high fructose corn syrup laden with red dye number 5?" You might as well have strapped on a feed bag full of white granulated sugar. You couldn't pay me to drink that stuff now (though there remains a strong attraction to the red mustache).

Standing with a cool cup of sugary liquid death in my hand, I couldn't imagine how some adults could drink wine. Disgusting! What were they thinking? But now that I've matured, kind of, I love cabernets, malbecs, and pinot noirs.

My point is that even if you're convinced you'll never like certain things, at some point they might become desirable. Because of sin, the things that lead us to God are contrary to our current, fallen state. They're acquired tastes. My eldest daughter once took a sip of my wine and emphatically declared, "I don't like acquired tastes!" None of us do in the beginning. That's why they're called "acquired tastes," silly.

Unless you were one of those scary kids who matured really fast — you know, had a beard and a voice resembling a tuba in fifth grade — unless you were one of them, most guys only pretend to like their first beer. You'd much rather be drinking that strawberry-kiwi wine cooler — that is, alcoholic Kool-Aid — at your first adult party. But as time goes by and you keep forcing yourself to drink it because your manhood is on the line, beer no longer tastes like dirty dishwater. You actually start to desire that creamy, frothed mug filled with a smooth Belgian White. Now there's nothing better.

It's the same with growth in the spiritual life, especially suffering. Because it is leading us to God and we know it, we begin to desire it, because God is everything!

Somebody Turn On the Lights

As you develop and realize the shallowness of living only for this world and are striving for holiness and virtue; engaging in deep, regular prayer; and feeling the presence of God — you suddenly come to a crisis. It's perhaps the most difficult thing you will experience in your spiritual journey: the transition of the soul from the Illuminative Way into the Unitive Way, the highest spiritual stage. This is the final rite of passage into spiritual adulthood.

Why is it a crisis? St. John of the Cross says it's the purification of the spirit, popularly known as "the dark night of the soul."[11] I know. It even sounds scary. It's like something Vincent Price or Darth Vader should be introducing.

The dark night of the soul is a feeling of abandonment by God experienced by people who have reached the higher stages of prayer and the spiritual life. It's the final purging process, during which we learn to seek God, no matter how distant he seems. Whereas in the earlier stages of spiritual growth a strong sense of God's presence is typically felt, in the dark night he disappears. He's not gone, but you can't feel him anymore — at all.

John of the Cross knew what he was talking about, too. "The Dark Night of the Soul" is a poem he wrote while imprisoned by his own brother monks who were opposed to reforms he was attempting to make in the Carmelite order. The poem describes a soul's journey to union with God and the dark trials it must endure while detaching from this world.

The dark night of the soul is all about cleaning house — getting rid of anything and everything in our lives opposed to God. You can't move new furniture in until you've moved the old out. Because of our weaknesses, we can't do this ourselves. God has to be involved. His purification of our soul happens on so deep a level we're not even aware of his movements. For this reason, this transition stage of the spiritual life is often called the passive purification of the spirit.

The paradox of this purification is that, on one hand, we've progressed far enough in the spiritual life to have experienced the mad desire for God, like the bride awaiting her lover in Song of Songs. (Check it out. Way better than a Harlequin romance.) We know he is everything, all we want. "O guiding night! O night more lovely than dawn! O night that has united the Lover with his beloved," cries John.[12]

On the other hand, the overwhelming sentiment of the dark night is one of total aridity of spirit. There's a lack of desire to love, gnawing emptiness, and a sense of abandonment by God. Of course, the reality is that God never abandons us. The reason it feels this way is because our impurities are being exposed to the purity of God. It's like walking out of a pitch-black theater into the bright sun and being forced to squint or shade your eyes. For a time it feels as if the sun is against us, when in reality we just haven't yet fully adjusted to its illumination.

The dark night exposes the soul to the white-hot love of God. Our own filth causes us great misery and "the soul understands distinctly that it is worthy neither of God nor of any creature," says St. John. He indicates that people suffer interiorly so much at this stage that any "soul would consider death a relief."[13] It reminds one of David's wailing in Psalm 18, "The sighs of death encircled me, the sorrows of hell surrounded me, in my tribulation I cried out" (18:5-6).[14]

"Well, thanks for the pep talk, Matt! Can't wait to get there! (C'mon guys, let's blow this joint.)" Hold on, partner. I'm not finished. Or rather, God's not finished. Like a log being consumed and transformed by fire, this passive purification in the dark night is transforming us into the likeness of God. Don't be afraid because this is it, the final transformation before encountering his glory. When you get right down to it, this purification is the beginning of the process completed in purgatory, which ends with entrance into the eternal bliss of full union with God.

Father Reginald Garrigou-LaGrange, the great Dominican spiritual writer, likens the dark night to the ascension of Christ. There were the poor apostles — intimate friends with Jesus for years, growing in understanding and love of the Lord. They heard powerful teaching. They saw miracles. Some were present at the Transfiguration and beheld Our Lord's glory. At the pinnacle of their lives they even saw the Resurrected Christ. Everything was great! He was the real deal, and they were part of his team. It couldn't get any better. But forty days after he rose from the dead he disappeared into the clouds (see Acts 1:9).

That wasn't the end of the road for the apostles, though. Their experience of God didn't end in spiritual darkness and abandonment. Similarly, we don't stay in the dark night forever. This third conversion of the spiritual life leads to an even deeper relationship with God.

Father Garrigou-LaGrange points out that nine days after the Ascension the apostles entered into an entirely new relationship with Christ, a union with him that changed everything. At Pentecost, the Holy Spirit descended, transforming them into spiritual dynamos. They entered more deeply into the mysteries of God and the supernatural life. They preached with abandon. They performed miracles. They prayed with power. Thousands came to God through their work, and they built the Catholic Church. The apostles wielded great power because their love of God had exploded through an encounter with his Spirit. They belonged completely to him and were full to the brim with life.

This is like the Unitive Way, says Father Garrigou-LaGrange. We have entered into a new dimension in our bond with God. A man and woman enter more deeply into relationship through marriage, and in a similar way we are unified with God in an ecstasy that makes everything else pale in comparison. We come to understand more profoundly the mysteries of God and experience him in a way that often defies description. Why? Because we're tasting eternity.

This is the final death of the "old man" and the putting on of the "new man," described by St. Paul in Colossians 3:9-10. The dark night of the soul is the trial through which we finally learn to love God with our whole heart, whole soul, and whole strength.

The life that follows in this final stage of spiritual development is nothing short of spiritual bliss. We've found the peace that passes all understanding, the unspeakable joy of encountering God. We revel in his love for us as his children, secure in the knowledge that no matter what happens all is well. We've moved into a new state of being, with which nothing else but heaven itself can compete. This is what it's all about. This is what we're striving for. And prayer is the key that unlocks the door to this new life.

CHAPTER 5

How Does Prayer Work?

"I wonder if this will work," I thought, steadily rubbing the beads dangling between my fingers. I wasn't holding my breath. Standing in the corner of a deserted terminal at O'Hare Airport in Chicago, I was lamenting (maybe even cursing) the storms in Germany driving my present distress. With my now useless standby ticket clutched firmly in hand, I had just watched all the booked passengers on the last flight of the day disappear down the jetway. The only other people in sight were the two friends with whom I was traveling.

Friends they might be, but I wasn't particularly interested in their company at the moment. Not that they cared. It made little difference to them where they made googly-eyes at each other. Who could blame them? They were in love, even if they weren't officially dating. (They're now married with five children and godparents to my firstborn, as my wife and I are to theirs.) I was a bit more perturbed than they at the prospect of spending the night in Chicago and doing this all over again. Weather forecasts going forward didn't bode well, and once again we wouldn't have guaranteed seats. Hence, the rosary.

I don't remember what decade I was on when I saw one of the gate agents emerge from the tunnel with a harried look on his face. Apparently I wasn't the only one stressed out by the number of people needing to get on that jet. Smiling through my angst as he passed by, I sardonically asked, "You wouldn't happen to have any more seats on that plane, would you?" To my shock, he stopped cold and practically yelled, "How many of you are there?"

"Three!" I practically shouted back.

"Grab your bags and follow me!"

Seized with excitement and waving like an overzealous prom queen, I screamed at my lovesick(ening) companions to follow. We rushed to the ticket counter, dragging more than pulling our luggage. Like a jackhammer, the agent's fingers pounded away on the computer keyboard taking our information. To my recollection, he never even looked at us, being so intent on the screen. After the fastest check-in ever recorded in airline history, we raced down the jetway, boarding passes waving wildly in hand. It was a miracle. The last three seats were ours. My prayers had worked! But it got even better.

Stepping aboard the huge airplane, we were promptly informed of the seating arrangements. "There are two seats together in coach and one in business class," said the stewardess. There was no question in anyone's minds who was going where.

"See you guys later," I said, heading toward the front of the plane. Smiles on the other two faces greeted my wave, and they happily trundled off to their adjoining seats farther back. Stowing my luggage in the overhead bin, I gratefully planted myself in the oversized leather seat next to another gentleman.

"Thank you, God!" I silently prayed, settling in. Moments later a flight attendant approached.

"Hello, gentlemen!" she said with a big smile. "I'd like to take your dinner order. The main course for our flight this evening is a choice between chicken and filet mignon." Looking at me, she asked, "Mr. Johnson?"

"Mr. Johnson couldn't make it," I replied with my own broad smile. "But Mr. Leonard will have the filet."

What's the Point?

It's not easy to answer the question of exactly how prayer works. I've often found myself wondering about it — and not just when I'm trying to get on a flight. There are many facets to the question, but unlike the popularity of professional wrestling, it's not a pure mystery.

The first thing to realize is that prayer isn't magic whereby we manipulate God. It doesn't change the will of God. We can't somehow twist his arm and get him to do something simply by asking or going through some prayer ritual. The *Catechism* tells us God is "unchangeable" (202). Scripture agrees. "Jesus Christ is the same yesterday and today and for ever," says Hebrews 13:8.

We also can't forget that God is the force behind everything. There is nothing that exists apart from him, and nothing happens except through his power. And I don't mean just big stuff. The fact that you can breathe, eat a jelly donut, or read this book is only because God gives you the ability. As Jesus said, "Apart from me you can do nothing" (Jn 15:5).

This raises an obvious question. If we can't change God's mind, and everything depends on him, then why in the world do we pray in the first place? The quick answer is that's the way God set it all up. It's how he designed our conversation with him. But let's take a deeper look.

Before we get to the heart of the answer, we need to talk about two complex topics: grace and freedom. I'm going to tell you right off the bat that these two are toughies, and it can be difficult to grasp exactly how they relate to one another. That relationship has been debated more hotly than the question of who is the best James Bond. (Sean Connery, of course). As finite beings, most of whom have trouble with basic algebra, we have to accept there's a mystery associated with the interaction of grace and freedom. Nevertheless, there are some things we can nail down that will help us perceive the inner dynamic of prayer.

Grace

There are two types of grace: sanctifying and actual. Sanctifying grace is what saves us. It's the kind of grace we receive in the sacraments beginning with baptism, the indwelling of God in our lives, the seed of eternal life. Sanctifying grace is what we lose through mortal sin. Without it, we are spiritually dead.

Actual grace is the kick in the pants God gives us so that we'll move toward him, so we'll turn and receive sanctifying grace. Even after we receive sanctifying grace and are "right with God," we continue to receive actual graces from God. We get them until the day we die. They are little "holy helps" that lead us to perfection and help prevent the loss of sanctifying grace. I like to imagine actual graces as little arrows constantly bombarding my body, helping point me in the right direction.

It's a pretty sweet deal when you think about it. God not only offers us salvation through his grace, he even gives grace to help us receive grace. It's like taking a test where our hands are actually guided to mark the appropriate box while the answers are being whispered in our ear. "How come then," you wonder, "we aren't all getting straight A's?" (I'm assuming that's a rhetorical question.) Read on.

Because we are free — and stubborn — we can still resist actual graces. But God continues to gently and patiently move us toward the right answer, toward himself. In fact, God has taken patience to a new level. Think about it. Any sin is an incredible offense against God. He hates it. But since we can do nothing without him, the only way we can commit sin is if he gives us the ability to do so. Remember, without his grace we would simply cease to be. God is such a loving, patient Father that he allows us to offend him if we so choose. He patiently waits for us — and provides more grace — to realize our job is not resistance but cooperation with the actual graces he provides.

Of course, this idea that we can resist God brings up some interesting stuff. As we've noted a couple of times already, we can't do anything without him. How we get to heaven is obviously no exception.

Augustine once said, "In the business of salvation all is the gift of God."[15] That even includes our cooperation. There is nothing in the process of getting to heaven that is exclusively ours. If the origin of our power to commit even sinful actions comes from God, how much more are the good works we perform finding their origin in him? There are no two ways about it. God is everything. And here's the kicker. Since he's the source of everything, God already knows what we're going to do from all eternity. He holds everything in existence and so has always known what is going to happen. He is the origin of everything, except evil.

"Wait a second, Matt!" you exclaim. (Keep it down, man, I'm right here.) "What about our free will? Can't we choose what we want or don't want?" The answer is "yes, in a sense." But don't forget that the only reason we have a free will is because God gave it to us. (Trippy, I know.) Created in God's image, we are free. It's one of the greatest gifts we've received. But just because we're free doesn't mean we're the *cause* of our freedom. A teenager may be free to go out on Saturday night with his buddies, but only because his parents allow him. They are more the cause of his freedom than he is. He just exercises it — until he's caught smoking with his buddies.

The actual graces God gives don't destroy our human liberty. God can gently move us without violating our free will because, as Thomas Aquinas says, he is closer to us than we are to ourselves.[16] God didn't make us robots. Rather, he made us in his image and invites us to himself. He only wants our *free* response, which we can give through the help of the grace he provides. "We also work," says Augustine, "but we are only collaborating with God who works, for his mercy has gone before us" (CCC 2001).

Working for a Living

This is pretty heady stuff, I know. But it's important to understand at least something of the topic of grace and freedom because it has direct consequences on how you get to heaven. While God is the power behind everything good and he wills that all be saved (see 1 Tm 2:4), that doesn't give us a license to simply go through life doing whatever we want. Salvation is a gift he freely offers, but we must work it out in "fear and trembling" (Phil 2:12). In other words, God isn't forced to fix us when we freely choose our own destruction, even though he often does. He created us with freedom and respects our choices, and there are consequences if we abuse it. Assuming he is going to save us no matter what we do is the sin of presumption. It would be like jumping into the deep end of a deserted swimming pool, clad with concrete boots, expecting someone to come to the rescue. Not a wise move.

Since we have that (kind of) straightened out, let's return to the original question. If God doesn't change and everything good ultimately comes from him, through his power, why should we pray? It's actually a pretty easy answer: cause and effect.

We all recognize and accept that in the natural world God has set things up in a particular way, with certain rules that govern our existence. If you drop a rock, it will fall. If you eat too much candy, you'll get sick. To reap a harvest, you must first sow the seed. The same kinds of rules apply to the supernatural world. To reap a spiritual harvest, you must first sow the spiritual seed. Prayer is that seed. It's a primary cause that produces effects of grace. It sets things in motion.

Prayer is necessary and efficacious because that's the way God wants it. It's a homage to his providence. In fact, prayer acknowledges that there is a God and that we are governed by a divine Being who is deeply interested in the affairs of our life. It seeks a power that is beyond that of men. Prayer can obtain and achieve that which only God can give. You just have to have a little faith.

Faith

There was a guy in my high school who started to lose his hair early. Speaking as a follicly challenged man in my mid-forties, I can empathize. But losing it so early is a whole different ballgame. It just shouldn't be that way. He stated during a prayer service that his hair would come back because he had faith God would heal his cue-ball-esque appearance. All he needed, he thought, was enough faith. After all, he reasoned, Jesus told the disciples they could move mountains if they had enough faith (see Mt 17:20; Mk 11:23). Not surprisingly, he is balder today than he was twenty-five years ago.

On the other hand, there are plenty of examples from Scripture where God rewards a person's faith. In Matthew's Gospel, two blind men approach Jesus seeking to be healed. "'Do you believe that I am able to do this?' They said to him, 'Yes, Lord.' Then he touched their eyes, saying, 'According to your faith let it be done to you.' And their eyes were opened" (9:28-30). Similar scenes include the healing of the hemor-rhaging woman (see Mk 5:25-34), the healing of the Canaan-ite woman's daughter (Mt 15:21-28), the healing of the ten lepers (Lk 17:11-19), and the list goes on. All asked for heal-ing and received it based on their faith. So what's the deal? How does faith work?

Can You Hear Me Now?

The *Catechism* tells us "*faith is a gift of God, a supernatural virtue infused by him*" (153). It's a gift solely given through grace. We may not be able to conjure it up on our own, but we sure do know how to squash it. How many times have you heard someone say, "Well, all we can do now is pray," as if it's the last resort? Rather than the last thing we do, it should be the first. "But why," you ask, "doesn't God always answer? In fact, there are lots of times when I pray and get no response, Matt."

Isn't it interesting that we never wonder if God hears our adoration and praise, but we always question whether he heard our latest request because we don't see immediate results, or results at all. It's pretty silly when you think about it. We're basically treating God as if he's a divine egomaniac who only hears what strokes him.

On the other hand, we have to admit it's sometimes hard to believe God has heard our petitions because we're so geared for empirical data. We want visible results, hard facts. Rain down some fire! Shake the earth! Show me the money! And even when that happens, we often don't believe. The Israelites cried out to God for deliverance, and through a most incredible series of events including plagues, the parting of the Red Sea, the destruction of the entire Egyptian army, pillars of cloud and fire, and more, he did as they requested. Even after all that, they thought he was going to leave them to starve to death in the wilderness. So he gave them manna, bread from heaven, every day for forty years. Even so, the Israelites' story (and ours) is one of constant lack of faith. We find it so hard to believe he's going to come through yet again.

Regardless of what God has often demonstrated for all to see, at its core "faith is the assurance of things hoped for, the conviction of things not seen" (Heb 11:1). Faith is supernatural, going beyond this visible world. As such, it frequently tests us. God often requires patience. (He's never late, but he's seldom early.) In fact, sometimes what God asks us to believe appears downright nuts in the eyes of the world, and maybe ours, too.

The first example would be good old Noah and his ridiculous-looking ark. We all know that story. But imagine what the Canaanites manning the parapets of the fortress city of Jericho thought when they saw the Israelites marching around the city in the Book of Joshua, Chapter 6. Through Joshua, God had ordered them to circle the city once a day for six days. The only thing to be heard was the blowing of trumpets by the seven priests who led the procession. The people weren't even to speak. If there was any trash-talking, it only came from the soldiers in the city. ("Hey, Israelite! You walk like an Egyptian!" Cue The Bangles.) You can't blame them, I guess. What else did they have to do? What kind of a siege was this, anyway?

Shockingly, given their track record, the Israelites did exactly what God wanted them to do. The results were spectacular. On the seventh day, per God's instructions, the people joined their voices to blaring trumpets, shouting to the Lord. The rest is history, familiar to everybody. Even Elvis (before he left the building) sang: "Joshua fit the battle of Jericho. And the walls come tumbling down." (Thank you. Thank you very much.)

The bottom line is: When we are faithful to what God asks, he delivers. It's that simple. "But, Matt," you say, "there's this one thing I've been asking about for a long time, and it still hasn't happened. Why not?"

One of the reasons we don't always get what we want is because often we're asking for the wrong things. That sweet new car or coveted promotion may look good, but are they good for you? Perhaps you'll become unbearable to others as you obsess over your car — like guys who use a Q-tip when applying the finishing touches to a wax job. Maybe that new job you really want will have you working so hard you forget where you live. Perhaps that's why our hot line from heaven has yet to ring. God's not going to do anything that isn't good for us. Like any good father, he is always seeking what's best for our eternal salvation, not just happiness in the here and now. Ask yourself if you're requesting the right things. In fact, go beyond that. Examine your motive for asking.

If you ever turn on a television, odds are you'll come across a crime drama in your channel-surfing. Set locations differ, but they're all essentially the same. A bad guy did something bad, and the good guys have to figure it out and catch him. Looking at potential suspects, the lead cop inevitably turns to his team and declares, "We need a motive, people!"

Motives aren't just relevant in crime solving. They're vitally important in the spiritual life, too. As Christ says in the beatitudes, "Blessed are the pure in heart" (Mt 5:8). God wants to give us good gifts, but he wants us to ask for the right reasons. He doesn't desire divided hearts (see Jas 4:4). Before asking God for something in prayer, ask yourself why you're asking. Check your motive.

"I hear you, Matt. I need to check my motive and ask for the right reason. But that's just it. Sometimes my prayer wasn't answered even when I prayed for something I knew was good." I know. It's happened to me, too. There are times we're asking for something that seems right and we still don't get what would appear to be the best answer from a natural perspective. For five years I continually prayed for a miraculous healing of my mom's cancer to no avail. She suffered terribly and eventually passed away. For a time, I struggled with why God didn't answer my prayer. The fact of the matter is he did, just not the way I wanted. In his perfect will, it was her time to go "home." I had to reconcile myself to the fact that God's answer is always best, even if it doesn't appear that way.

Look at Christ. Facing a horrific crucifixion, Jesus himself asked the Father to "let this cup pass from me" (Mt 26:39). His humanity recoiled at the thought of what was coming and naturally desired to be spared. We'd all be praying the same thing, I'm sure! And yet, he wasn't delivered.

"Well, Matt," you point out, "he had to go through with it. Otherwise we wouldn't be saved!" Easy to say that now, isn't it? We have the benefit of looking back and knowing from divine revelation what it was all about. God has that benefit all the time. He always sees the big picture. He answered his Son's prayer, just not in the manner most comfortable for Jesus' humanity. He knew what was best from a divine perspective for our eternal salvation.

The key to getting the "right" answer every time we pray is pretty simple: Learn to pray for the things God wants. Immediately after asking the Father for deliverance, Jesus prayed, "Nevertheless, not as I will, but as thou will" (Mt 26:39). Like the Son, we have to get to the point where we accept that Father knows best. Just look at the results of his (lack of) response to Jesus: eternal salvation for the world! While from a human perspective it seems unconscionable he would let his Son suffer and die, the Father was preparing the greatest gift he could possibly give the world and the greatest glory for his Son, whom he "highly exalted" and gave "the name which is above every name" (Phil 2:9).

This brings up an interesting point. Often we don't ask for enough when we pray. We're thinking too small. But our Father in heaven "desires to do something even greater" than what you want says the *Catechism* (2737). This doesn't just apply to huge issues, but even the most ordinary of life's events. I only prayed for a seat on the plane to Europe, the bare minimum. I'd have gladly taken one right by the bathroom next to the one-year-old twins cutting teeth. But God gave me a quiet seat more comfortable than the recliner in my living room, and a great dinner to boot. And if he cares that much about my getting a seat on a plane, how much more does he care about the deeper needs and issues in life?

Thy Will Be Done

If you're anything like me, it's more likely you're asking for the wrong thing instead of not enough. That's why conforming our will to God's is so important. But sometimes in so doing we forget the bigger picture. Some people spend a lot of time trying to figure out what God wants them to do in every little situation. They fret and fuss and worry about spiritually unimportant matters. ("O Father in heaven, should I buy the red one or the blue one?") Not only will this never get anything done, but it isn't necessary. Why? First of all, God isn't some vindictive cuss waiting to whack us upside the head when we make a "wrong" decision. Rather, he's our Father who loves us. Not every decision is life or death.

If my son were to tell me, "Dad, I either want to be an astronaut or a writer," I would first thank God he didn't say politician. Then I would figure out how I could help him achieve his dreams — within reason, since they'll probably change more often than a chameleon on a kaleidoscope. That's what good fathers do. If we're really trying to do his will, not only is God going to respect our decision; he's going to make it work. For "we know that in everything God works for good with those who love him, who are called according to his purpose" (Rom 8:28).

God is always willing to write straight with our crooked lines. So we can relax, especially when we're dealing with issues that aren't intrinsically good or evil. Should I take that new job? Should I buy that other car? Butterfinger or Snickers? Talk to God if necessary and make your best choice. (Butterfinger every time.)

And if you want to have the best chance of knowing what God wants — how to write with the straightest line possible from the very beginning — there's one simple rule that works every time: get close to God. It's that easy — and that hard! I can yell at the top of my lungs for my kids to clean their rooms, but if they've conveniently left the building with Elvis, they can't hear my voice. As our Father's children we have to get close so we can hear what he's saying. If you put your relationship with God first, you'll be more tuned in to what he desires for your life. You'll be able to hear what he's telling you to do. And nobody else is looking out for your interests the way he is.

Ultimately, we know our prayers work because of Jesus Christ. God hears us because Christ "prays in us and with us" (CCC 2740). We can boldly go to the Father because we are "sons in the Son," adopted children united to Christ through the sacraments. As long as we're joined to him, Jesus makes our prayers work for our eternal good.

CHAPTER 6

Talking to God

Words are powerful. The old adage "the pen is mightier than the sword" is assuredly true. Words can start wars, ensure peace, or get my dog to roll over ... sometimes. Words can even create relationships. Unless you used one of those "check this box if you'll marry me" notes, one simple word — "yes" — signals an engagement. Two not-so-simple words — "yes, dear" — ensure a happy marriage.

Of course, it's God himself who really proves the power of words. In the beginning he "spoke, and it came to be" (Ps 33:9). Starting with "let there be light," the whole universe came into existence simply through the power of God's words. That's some pretty impressive speech.

In the New Testament we discover even more about the power behind God's words. "In the beginning was the Word, and the Word was with God, and the Word was God" (Jn 1:1). Not only that, but "the Word became flesh and dwelt among us" (Jn 1:14). In other words, the Word is a person. It's Jesus Christ, the Creator and Redeemer of the whole world. He is the Word. And we are created in his image (see Gn 1:26-27).

Chitchat

People are talkers. All over the world millions upon millions of conversations are taking place right this moment. In just about any public place aside from a library or cemetery the din of voices is the dominant feature. To converse is human. And in this regard, some people are more human than others.

I once asked my brother-in-law, a Protestant pastor, to say a blessing over a family meal at my house. Having prayed publicly on many occasions, he's quite eloquent. On this day, however, his abilities were not appreciated by my two-year-old daughter. Being used to the traditional "Bless us, O Lord, and these thy gifts" prayer, she lost patience forty-five seconds into my brother-in-law's longish, "from the hip" prayer. Upon his taking a breath, she cried out, "Amen!" effectively signaling the beginning of the meal.

Long prayers are one thing, but all too often we talk about the wrong kinds of things in general conversation. Gossip and slander, for example, are two things God can't stand (see Rom 1:29 and Ps 101:5). A lying tongue is an "abomination," and you deceive yourself if you think you're religious but can't "bridle" your tongue, says the Bible (see Prv 6:16-17 and Jas 1:26). James goes so far as to warn, "The tongue is a fire ... staining the whole body" if we're not careful (Jas 3:6). One careless whisper can destroy a friendship or someone's reputation. Worse yet, words can destroy your relationship with God.

Even so, talking is essential to how people relate to one another. Words are essential to communicating thought. Unless it's early morning on a school day, my kids don't just stare at me hoping I'll understand when they want more milk or cereal. Before they can even form coherent words, children attempt to communicate through sounds. It's natural. Replete with lungs, vocal chords, and (big) mouths, we have the God-given ability to express ourselves in a physical way. We aren't pure spirits like angels. Nor are we bumps on a log with no spiritual soul. We are a combo platter of body and spirit with the God-given ability to communicate externally. And the person with whom we most need to speak is God.

Forms of Prayer

Vocal prayer, the kind with which most of us are familiar, is a vital part of our relationship with God. As mentioned back in Chapter 2, there are several different forms vocal prayer can take. The *Catechism* lists adoration as the first kind of prayer because it acknowledges that we are creatures before our Creator and "exalts the greatness of the Lord who made us" (2628; see Ps 95:1-6). Adoration is due to God alone because only he made us and sets us free from evil.

While adoration has pride of place, when most of us think of prayer, the first kind that comes to mind is petition. That's because it seems we're always asking God for something. In truth, we have to. If man hadn't fallen, says Spiritan priest and author Father Edward Leen, "our utterances would mainly consist of words of praise and adoration and worship."[17] But as it is, "all our dealings with God must have a background of pleading in them."[18] Only God can give us what we need.

When things aren't going so well, we turn to another kind of prayer — intercession — which is done on behalf of another person. Intercessory prayer is really powerful because it "leads us to pray as Jesus did" (CCC 2634). In other words, it's a twofer, helping us because we're acting like Christ, and helping the other person for whom we're praying. Intercession is so important that the Holy Spirit himself "intercedes for us through wordless groans" (Rom 8:26, New International Version) — which sounds like an effective way to clear a seat or two in a crowded adoration chapel.

If our priorities are straight, thanksgiving, a third kind of vocal prayer, should be one of our most natural forms. After all, God is good and offers us salvation even though we deserve death. That's something to be thankful for in my opinion. And he gives us many more reasons to be thankful in this life as well, beginning with the Eucharist. Every Eucharistic liturgy is a "sacrifice of thanksgiving to the Father" (CCC 1360). Indeed, *eucharistia*, the Greek word from which we get "Eucharist," means "thanksgiving."

Praise, the last form of vocal prayer mentioned in the *Catechism*, recognizes that "God is God," and gives him glory simply for who he is (see 2639). We especially like to praise people after they've done something good. (Toddlers undergoing potty-training are the most praised people on earth.) But God is worthy of praise simply by virtue of being God. Progress in prayer always entails the prayer of praise. It's foundational. In fact, it "embraces the other forms of prayer and carries them toward" God (CCC 2639).

The Bible Tells Me So

If you've ever perused the Bible for any length of time, you've probably noticed vocal prayer is everywhere. Their last encounter wasn't exactly an International Coffee moment, but Adam and Eve talked with God in the Garden of Eden. Noah and God spent a fair bit of time conversing about the weather. Abraham even tried to negotiate fire insurance for Sodom and Gomorrah with God (but the premium was too expensive). This kind of thing happens throughout the Old Testament. Jacob, Moses, David, the prophets, and many others speak with God about all kinds of stuff.

Of course, in the New Testament, people didn't stop praying. Numerous stories of the apostles, Our Lady, St. Paul, and many others praying or referring to prayer abound. On the eve of Pentecost, the beginning of the Church, many "with one accord devoted themselves to prayer" (Acts 1:14). And they didn't stop once the Spirit came. Acts tells us the three thousand new converts "held steadfastly to the apostles' teaching and fellowship, to the breaking of the bread and to the prayers" (2:42). Jesus had taught them well.

When you read through the Gospels, you simply can't escape the great importance Christ placed on prayer. Right before all the big events of his life — choosing the apostles, the Transfiguration, and his Passion, to name but a few — he's talking it over with his Father. While still Cardinal Joseph Ratzinger, Pope Benedict XVI wrote that "according to the testimony of Holy Scripture, the center of the life and person of Jesus is his constant communication with the Father."[19]

Now ask yourself this. If talking with God was so critical to all the important characters in the Bible, not to mention the incarnate Second Person of the Trinity, how important should it be to us? Yep. Really, *really* important. So let's delve into a little more detail about this "essential element of the Christian life" (CCC 2701).

Straight from the Heart

Since we are a union of body and soul, it's important to remember that vocal prayer isn't just a physical exercise. You can flap your yap all you want, but if your words aren't coming from the heart you're not praying. Even Mr. Golden Tongue himself, St. John Chrysostom, said, "Whether or not our prayer is heard depends not on the number of words, but on the fervor of our souls" (CCC 2700).

Vocal prayer must be an expression of our interior life. One of the reasons the Psalms are so powerful is that their author is letting it all hang out: "I am weary with my moaning; every night I flood my bed with tears; I drench my couch with my weeping" (6:6). This guy (King David) obviously had some serious problems. Perhaps a few sessions with a good counselor or spiritual director might have been in order. Regardless, he didn't hold back from telling God exactly how he felt.

One of the lessons we can learn from David and others is that sometimes our vocal prayers are too sanitary or weak. We hold back, thinking this or that issue wouldn't be proper to talk about with God. I'm not saying we should treat God as a gossip partner or blithely discuss immorality with him in prayer, but we need to remember just who he is. He is the God who gave us life. He is the God who knows exactly who we are and what he wants us to be. He is the God who is our Father.

Father God

Prayer isn't simply the conversation of a created person with the Creator. It is the personal "conversation of a child with its heavenly Father," says the great abbot and spiritual writer Blessed Columba Marmion. We can't forget we remain creatures, but God gave us the dignity of being part of his family through his Son. Because of his Incarnation, Passion, death and resurrection, we now relate to God through Jesus Christ. This understanding is a must if we are going to comprehend prayer.

And when we say that "God is Father," we're not making an analogy. As I previously noted, God isn't *like* a family, he isn't *like* a father. It's who he is. It's his personal name, his identity.[20] My name is Matt. It's who I am. Well, God is Father. It's who he is. Jesus shows us that "Father" is God's name by virtue of his own identity as "Son." But he also explicitly reveals the Father as such. He told his disciples to baptize converts "in the name of the Father and of the Son and of the Holy Spirit" (Mt 28:19).

Referencing Pope Benedict XVI, theologian Scott Hahn points out that while we have all kinds of other titles for God like "Creator," "Lawgiver," and "Physician," those titles only apply *after* he has created, given the law, and healed people. But he is "Father forever, because He eternally generates the Son, and together they breathe forth the Spirit, the bond of their love."[21] Put simply, there was never a time when he was not Father.

Why am I putting such emphasis upon God's fatherhood? Because Jesus did. He calls God "Father" seventeen times in the Sermon on the Mount alone. Blessed Columba Marmion said that God's fatherhood is the fundamental dogma which precludes all others.[22] In other words, everything we believe starts with the understanding that God is our Father … which presents some challenges.

Grasping God as Father is difficult for a lot of people because, let's face it, human fathers are just that — human. Even dads who take their paternity seriously make mistakes. Speaking as the father of five children (so far), I can tell you I fall flat on my fatherly face every day in dealings with my little rug rats. But God isn't like me, or any other human father. In fact, the *Catechism* tells us he is more *unlike* human fathers than like them, and we had better be careful not to think otherwise. "God our Father transcends the categories of the created world. To impose our own ideas in this area 'upon him' would be to fabricate idols to adore or pull down" (CCC 2779).

God's fatherhood is different because he isn't an earthly father. He is "Our Father who art in heaven" (Mt 6:9). To understand the depth of his love for us, his family, we have to stop imposing our false notions of father upon him. Many people endure seriously wounded relationships with their earthly fathers, or perhaps no relationship at all, so this is really hard. But it doesn't do God justice to equate him with those who might have failed us. And doing so keeps us from recognizing who we are in Christ Jesus — true children of God who can address the Father with all the familiarity of the Son. That's why the most perfect prayer ever designed is the one Jesus taught us, the Our Father.

The Perfect Prayer

Every Christian knows the Our Father by heart. At least I thought so until I realized my two-year-old daughter thought it ended with "deliver us from Nemo." Continuing the tradition a few years later, my three-year-old son thought it was "deliver us from people." (Both translations have their merits.)

Whether or not all the words are always said correctly by children or adults, it remains the most famous vocal prayer in the world, and it was given to us by Christ himself. In the Gospel of Luke, a disciple rolls up to Jesus and simply says, "Lord, teach us to pray" (11:1). So Jesus obliges. And this wasn't some spontaneous, thrown-together prayer designed to make him look good in front of his followers, which is what I would probably do. Rather, this prayer is the key to worshiping the Father in "spirit and truth." It's the secret to holiness that teaches us who God really is; his will, his love, his mercy, and how we're supposed to treat others.[23]

The Lord's Prayer is the centerpiece of the Sermon on the Mount in Matthew and a summary of the whole Gospel. As St. Augustine said, search all the prayers of the Bible and "I do not think that you will find anything in them that is not contained and included in the Lord's Prayer" (CCC 2762).

Not only does it sum up the Gospel, it does what the disciple requested — teaches us to pray. St. Thomas Aquinas said, "This prayer not only teaches us to ask for things, but also in what order we should desire them" (CCC 2763). So let's take a little lesson in vocal prayer from the Master himself.

The first thing to note is the Our Father is made up of seven petitions that can be divided into two parts: those directed toward God, and those directed toward us and our needs. The direction of the petitions, starting with God, forces us to start where we are unaccustomed, outside ourselves. It turns our fallen, "natural" priorities upside down and reorients us to God.

The Lord's Prayer is unique because the Divine Son himself gave it to us and it is the prayer of God, but it is also the prayer of Jesus' human heart, which he shares with the rest of us. In other words, it's a perfect prayer bridge from humanity to divinity. And Jesus gives us not only the words, but the Spirit, to pray them. Praying in and through Jesus guarantees that our prayer gets to God, because he is "the one Word [God] always hears" (CCC 2769).

We Dare to Say: Our Father, Who Art in Heaven

I once heard Fr. Michael Scanlan, former president of Franciscan University of Steubenville, tell the story of a Muslim man he invited to attend Mass at the school. After watching the students move through the Communion lines and receive Our Lord in the Eucharist, the Muslim stated, "There's no way they actually believe that is God."

More than a little surprised, Father Scanlan asked, "Why not?"

"Because if they did, they would be crawling on their faces toward him," he responded.

What disturbed this Muslim, and has shocked many others, too, is the primary idea of the Lord's Prayer we've already discussed — God's fatherhood. How dare we be so familiar with the Almighty God who created everything? But that's the scandal of the Gospel. We are created to be part of the family of God in a real way. We don't just get a legal name change when we're initiated into the family through the sacraments. It's a *divine* adoption. We become what we were made to be. It's a whole new identity in Jesus Christ. This is real!

Of course, it's sometimes hard to grasp how he is "Our Father" in "heaven," totally beyond us in glory and honor and majesty, and yet with us at the same time. But he is. Every dad knows it's impossible to father from a distance. Our Father in heaven is always close by. He always hears our cry, "Abba! Father!"

Hallowed Be Thy Name

Every year, fathers all over the world receive new ties, mugs, and cards in celebration of Father's Day. (I recently received an "I Am Your Father" Star Wars mug, which apparently makes me Darth Vader.) Mostly celebrated on the third Sunday of June, it's a day devoted to honoring the tough job of being a dad. I find it apropos that it is generally celebrated on the Lord's Day since our human fathers are an earthly image of our heavenly Father. In Germany, it's actually celebrated on Ascension Thursday.

So I ask, if earthly fathers deserve to be so honored, how much more our heavenly Father? That's what "hallowing" is all about. It means we give God glory and honor and praise in a way no one else deserves.

But it's still kind of funny we're the ones "hallowing," or blessing, the name of God. After all, we're the creatures and he's the Creator, right? We can't make God's name any more holy than it already is. So what's going on here?

The *Catechism* indicates that this petition is primarily expressing our desire to be holy through him. Through the sacraments we have become part of him. Baptized into the Father, Son, and Holy Spirit, we now bear the same name. We're really a part of his family, "immersed in the innermost mystery of his Godhead" (2807). In this petition, we're asking God to make us worthy of his name, to make us holy through his grace and love because we can't do it without him (Rv 15:4). That's it in a nutshell. That's why our petition to be holy "embodies all the others" of the Lord's Prayer (see CCC 2815).

Thy Kingdom Come

We have a room in my house called the "pink room," so called because of the carpeting. Before you begin questioning my manhood, allow me to explain. First of all, the technical color of the carpet is "dusty rose." (Yeah, that still doesn't work for me.) Second and more important, my little girls insisted we leave the pink carpet in place after moving in. Neutral colors were of no interest to them.

Piled high in one corner of our "pink room" is a mountain of princess dresses. Chiffon, velvet, lace, they all converge in a menagerie of royal girl-ness. It's all good until they dress up your only boy in so much purple velvet he resembles a living Infant of Prague. The simple fact is they love to be princesses, and in the years to come (I'm hoping thirty or so), they'll start longing for princes.

The point is that even in an age of republics and democracies the idea of kings, queens, princes, and princesses never really fades. And Christ uses the language of "kingdom" in his prayer. In fact, this kingdom is the primary theme of his entire ministry on earth as he refers over and over to "the kingdom of God" or "the kingdom of heaven."

In the historical sense, when Israel first became God's people, he was their king. But as time went by, they rejected God as ruler and demanded a human king like the other nations (see 1 Sm 8:5). God finally gave them what they wanted, which, after a false start with Saul, eventually led to the kingdom of David. It was the high point of Israel's history. God actually swore a covenant with David, a man after his own heart, promising David his son would be God's son and that David's kingdom would last forever (see Acts 13:22; 2 Sm 7:8-16). Though David's historical kingdom is the longest unbroken line of dynastic succession, it eventually was conquered and fell apart. So when it all went kaput, it appeared that God had broken his "forever" promise. Of course, God doesn't lie. His oath to David was eventually fulfilled in his Son, Jesus Christ.

In the very first verse of the New Testament, Matthew begins, "The book of the genealogy of Jesus Christ, the son of David." In other words, Jesus is of the royal line of David.

He's the heir to the throne. He was even born in the same city as King David — Bethlehem (which interestingly means "house of bread"). And as we said, his ministry was based on proclaiming that "the kingdom of heaven is at hand" (Mt 3:2). Through Christ, God has come to lead his people again. Even so, the Kingdom isn't fully here, though it's "been coming since the Last Supper," states the *Catechism*, "and, in the Eucharist, it is in our midst" (2816).

When we pray "Thy kingdom come" in the Lord's Prayer, we're asking for his kingdom to be made completely manifest. We're praying for our King, who was made flesh for our sake, to return in all his glory and reunite his kingdom.

Thy Will Be Done

This petition goes back to the discussion we had earlier about grace and freedom. God is unchangeable, and his will is going to be accomplished one way or the other. We can either accept it, a choice that leads to happiness, or reject it, a choice that leads to misery. It's that simple.

Still, I know some of you continue asking, "If it's ultimately going to happen one way or the other, why bother to pray?" As noted previously, part of the answer is that we don't totally understand the dynamic of prayer. God is unchangeable, and his will is going to be done one way or the other. But just as there are many ways to arrive at a particular destination, God's will can come to fruition in any number of ways. He is constantly working around our mistakes or capitalizing on our faithfulness. Prayer is part of that faithfulness.

Another aspect bears mentioning again. Prayer is the way God desires to communicate with his children. We are the children. God is the all-knowing, all-powerful, all-loving Father. Assuming he is the one who needs to bend to our will is the wrong perspective. It's basically saying God doesn't know what he's doing. The value of prayer is its power to conform us to God's perfect will. Why would we want to change perfection? Praying "Thy will be done" gives us grace to accept his will and the strength to follow it.

Recall that the point of this life is to be like Jesus Christ, who humbly gave himself over to the will of the Father, praying, "Not my will, but thine, be done" (Lk 22:42). By praying for God's will, we aren't resigning ourselves to an outcome over which we have no control. Rather, we're acting like children who trust their Father in heaven to always do what's best for them.

Give Us This Day Our Daily Bread

For a long time, this petition seemed to me to be a bit impertinent. Who am I to demand something from the God of the universe? It wasn't until I recognized my place as a true child of God that I could start to pray this petition with confidence. As Father, he promises to take care of all my needs, which I find pretty comforting.

Of course, this doesn't mean we can sit around all day playing video games or watching soap operas while eating coconut bonbons. An old saying often attributed to St. Ignatius Loyola tells us to "pray as if everything depended on God and work as if everything depended on you." And our prayers are not to solely revolve around our needs. We are God's hands and feet, so we must be instruments of God's provision for others who are in need.

But this petition isn't solely about material needs. At its heart lies a request for the "bread of life," the "medicine of immortality," the Eucharist, "without which we have no life within us" (Jn 6:35; CCC 2837). We also often overlook the fact that we're asking for "daily bread." Not so St. Ambrose:

But if it is "daily" bread, then why do you take it so infrequently? Take daily what will help you daily. And live so that you deserve to receive it daily. He who does not deserve to receive it daily does not deserve to receive it once a year.[24]

And Forgive Us Our Trespasses, As We Forgive Those Who Trespass Against Us

If I ever find my mind drifting off when praying the Our Father, this petition is the one that jolts me back to reality. We're basically saying, "God, don't forgive us unless we forgive everybody else who has ticked us off, stabbed us in the back, taken our stuff, or in any other manner wronged us." Yikes.

Don't forget, one of the primary ways we love God is through loving others. It's part two of Jesus' command to love God and love neighbor. If we can't open our hearts to forgive those who have harmed us, we can't be open to receive God's love either. There's no doubt this is hard, but it's not impossible. In asking God to forgive us, an exercise in humility, he gives graces to help us forgive others. God's cool that way. He knows we can't do it on our own, so he's constantly giving us help as he calls us to greater holiness.

And Lead Us Not into Temptation

This petition seems a bit odd at first blush, doesn't it? Why in the world would God lead us into temptation? That doesn't sound right! Relax. He doesn't. That's Satan's job. Even so, the Greek is a little hard to translate into English in a way that conveys the original meaning. To help provide context, the Letter of James says, "Let no one say when he is tempted, 'I am tempted by God'; for God cannot be tempted with evil and he himself tempts no one" (1:13). Jesus himself warned,

"Woe to the man by whom the temptation comes!" (Mt 18:7). Okay. So what's the deal with this petition?

Remember that God made us free, but freedom is a two-edged sword. On one hand, it allows us to freely give our love to God. On the other hand, it opens us up to temptation. We're not robots, so there are going to be times when we're faced with choosing either for God or against God. He doesn't create the temptation, but he permits it. Why?

It's kind of like that old saying, "Whatever doesn't kill you makes you stronger." I never really liked that, because it meant whatever I was dealing with could actually kill me; never a pleasant option. But the truth is, when tempted we come face-to-face with our weaknesses. We experience our total dependence upon God because we can't overcome it without him. And that's the beautiful thing in all of this. "God is faithful, and he will not let you be tempted beyond your strength, but with the temptation will also provide the way of escape, that you may be able to endure it" (1 Cor 10:13).

But be careful not to deliberately put yourself in a situation where you could fall into sin. Just because trial and temptation provide opportunities for growth and God permits them, we shouldn't seek them out. You'll have plenty of opportunities to be tested without seeking them. That's why we pray "lead us not into temptation."

But Deliver Us from Evil

In the final petition of the Our Father, we're not simply praying against evil in general. We're praying directly against the Evil One. We're basically asking God to keep the devil from throwing us any curveballs that would cause us to strike out and head to the spiritual bench. We need this petition, because while we know the final outcome has been decided through Christ, the devil still "prowls around like a roaring lion, seeking some one to devour" (1 Pt 5:8).

Finally, note that the entire Our Father is in the first person plural. It's not just you and God. We're praying to "our" Father for "us." We're praying with the rest of the Church, the rest of the Body of Christ, because we're all connected. That's why vocal prayer is used so frequently in the liturgy. It allows us to communicate with God as one voice. And when you're doing it correctly, with your heart fully engaged, vocal prayer can actually become meditation and contemplation.

CHAPTER 7

Meditation

My wife and I dated before the invention of smartphones and video chatting. But living in different cities forced us to rely on 1990s cutting-edge technology known as e-mail and "dumb" phones. We communicated a lot. But for the relationship to develop, we knew we'd have to actually spend time together, person to person. Any chance we got to actually see each other face-to-face was cause for rejoicing (and coiffing). It was during these times together that our relationship really grew.

Finally there came a time when I knew I would have to make a choice. Either I was going to leave my life in Chicago to pursue this relationship with the girl of my dreams, or I was going to spontaneously combust. Having never been attracted to the smell of burning flesh, particularly my own, I packed up and moved.

The life of prayer resembles human interaction. In order for us to grow in our relationship with God, we have to be present with him in an ever-growing, more personal way. While vocal prayer continues for the duration of our earthly lives, it isn't enough. To move into closer union with our Lord, we must engage in meditation — mental prayer. This is the next step in our maturation as children of God as we get to know our Father.

I have to admit to being a bit skeptical about meditation prior to becoming Catholic. To me, it smacked of non-Christian religions and people trying to find their inner something or other. But these are actually quite different from meditation. The *Catechism* teaches that meditation is nothing more than the quest of the mind seeking "to understand the why and how of the Christian life, in order to adhere and respond to what the Lord is asking" (2705).

Union with God is our final destiny, but meditation is where we begin to move into that union even now. And it's so important that St. Alphonsus Liguori declared, "Short of a miracle, a man who does not practice mental prayer will end up in mortal sin."[25] I don't know about you, but when I first read those words I got a little nervous. Unfortunately, he was just getting warmed up. Referencing St. Teresa of Ávila, he stated: "He who neglects mental prayer needs no devil to carry him to hell. He brings himself there with his own hands."[26]

As I said, I don't particularly enjoy the smell of burning flesh, so I've made meditation a staple of my daily activity, and you should, too. Everyone should. In his classic *The Spiritual Life*, Adolphe Tanquerey states that meditation is the "most effective means of assuring one's salvation."[27] It isn't an option. Meditation is a necessary part of our spiritual development and will save your skin, literally.

The "How-To" Meditate Part

So what is meditation? Basically, it's prayerful reflection on Our Lord aided by spiritual input. It's interior prayer where we revel in God's presence and allow him to seep not just into our bones, but into our marrow. "That sounds nice," you're thinking, "but how exactly do you do it? What does it look like, Matt?"

There's a lot to say about the ins and outs of meditative prayer, but since we only have a chapter, we'll stick with the basics. Frankly, that's all we need. Moving forward, we'll see that complicated explanations are too, well, complicated.

Because it's been around a long, long time, many different methods of meditation have developed over the centuries. Still, there is a kind of classic structure in the tradition of the Church. In my book *Louder Than Words: The Art of Living as a Catholic*, I list it out, using perhaps the most unhelpful acronym for meditation ever — "PRMRR." It stands for:

1. Pick a time and location
2. Recollect yourself
3. Meditate
4. Respond
5. Resolve

This simple list is the basic process of meditative prayer. Find yourself a place and time that allow you to quietly recollect yourself. I always encourage beginners to start with ten to fifteen minutes. It doesn't sound like much time on paper, but when you first begin it can be like watching turtles run a marathon.

Because of original sin we don't "naturally" take to spending quiet time with God. But the more you do it, the easier it becomes. After all, this kind of relationship with God is what we were made for. It's our divine destiny. So the more time we spend with God, stripping away the effects of sin, growing in virtue and love, the more the supernatural becomes the new "natural." Prayer becomes something we desire.

When practicing mental prayer, start by slowing down and focusing. All of our faculties — intellect, will, and memory — need to be fully engaged for this kind of prayer to be fruitful. You can't just bop in and bop out. This can require a Herculean effort even for those more inclined to a little slower pace than I am.

I tend to be an "A to B, there's nothing to see" kind of guy. I find out what has to be done, and I do it. Sometimes this is a virtue, and sometimes it's a vice. When it comes to mental prayer, it's both. My goal-driven personality generally rises to the challenge of making sufficient time for prayer, but

I have to guard against treating it as something to be checked off my spiritual to-do list, a faulty approach that can create serious problems with regard to talking to God.

Recollection is paramount. Just as you must be in the same place with someone to have a real face-to-face, we must put ourselves in the presence of God if we're going to have a truly personal conversation with him. I once read a spiritual writer who said even if the majority of your time in prayer is spent recollecting yourself, it's worth it. You simply can't pray if you're not present with the Lord.

There are many practical ways to accomplish recollection. But before we get there, we need to remember an important point. God is always with us. So, turning away from the world and putting ourselves in the presence of God isn't just something that happens when it's "go time" in our local adoration chapel or prayer corner. It's an attitude that must permeate every aspect of our lives long before we enter into active prayer. It's something we need to practice. And, again, it takes time. It's a habit that must be formed, just like bad habits take time to break.

Cold Turkey

Have you ever met someone who — cold turkey — gave up smoking? The process is generally not a pretty sight. Sure, there are a few hearty souls who seem to possess superhuman abilities in this regard, but for most smokers quitting is less appealing than a toothpick in the eye. They go from two packs a day of Lucky Strikes to feeling like they're sheer out of luck. (And they're not afraid to let the rest of us know how they feel.) Only a few can pull it off.

Most smokers stop in degrees. They begin by reducing the number of cigarettes per day, then slap on a couple of nicotine patches, and later graduate to furiously chomping nicotine gum until their jaw muscles resemble Arnold

Schwarzenegger's biceps. Finally, that overwhelming desire for another drag is vanquished and they're free! That's kind of what it's like when we decide to renounce the world to ensure our eternal health. It happens by degrees. And the more we reduce the amount of "world" in us, the more God fills us up, until we're finally free of our bondage to solely natural things.

Like everything else, this desire to free ourselves and move toward God is a grace. The very fact that a person begins to have a greater interest in spiritual things is already an indicator that God is at work in him. This is all important because deciding to renounce the world and embark upon spiritual study is what Father Edward Leen calls "remote preparation" for meditative prayer. It's a bit like that moment when the artificially colored *crème* of your oversized donut is squishing through your teeth and you finally realize, "This thing is going to kill me!" and vow, "Never again!" Ending your relationship with Little Debbie is remote preparation for physical health.

Spiritual health begins with turning away from sin and the distractions that keep us from God. This move prepares us for deeper prayer.

But for this to actually happen, and so that we don't fall back into the miry *crème* filling of this world, we must constantly seek more grace from God. Living off the fumes of our initial desire won't pay the spiritual bills. We have to continually fan the flames of love for God in our hearts. St. Teresa of Ávila warns not to slack off because "there are many things which may deprive us of this holy liberty of the spirit which we seek."[28]

In other words, it's not easy because we're as distractible as a little girl in a princess dress-up store with her daddy's credit card. We want everything on the rack and are drawn to the glitz and glitter of this world. We have to constantly stir up our wills so that our desire for God remains steadfast.

Mental prayer won't work unless we can sufficiently detach from this world. God moves us to pray, but it is a habit we must develop, a muscle we must strengthen.

Practically speaking, I've found that entering into some semblance of silence before I ever arrive at my local adoration chapel (where I often pray) always helps. Sometimes I'll pray a decade of the Rosary as I'm driving, or perhaps I just start talking to God. If I happen to have my silence-challenged children present in the car, I attempt to find a happy, quiet place deep inside the abyss of my interior self — which is nearly impossible.

When I can't start recollecting myself beforehand, I resort to other methods once in my prayer spot. Often I'll repeat the name of Jesus slowly and deliberately, thanking him for all he's done in my life. Other times I'll break open the Bible and read a passage that helps put me in the presence of the Lord. Most important, I ask the Holy Spirit to help me pray.

Listen Up

It's always a good idea to begin prayer with an act of humility so as to remember who we are before God. The Lord said to St. Catherine of Siena, "I am who I am, thou are she who is not."[29] Follow the act of humility by telling God you're sorry for your sin, and then tell him how much you love him. In other words, repent and adore. This is how to crush pride, the main obstacle to grace.

After you put yourself in the presence of God, meditation begins. This isn't chanting mantras or assuming the lotus position clad in a pair of Zubaz pants you found buried in your closet from the nineties. (Continue reading this book only after properly disposing of them and any unused weightlifting gloves you found under them.) Rather, it generally consists of slowly perusing a portion of spiritual reading like a saint's book, the Bible, or some other spiritual classic.

You can also meditate on an image, nature, or any number of other things that point to God, but we'll stick with books for explanatory purposes.

When choosing materials for meditation, remember that the focus is always Jesus Christ. Even when reading about saints, virtues, or other aspects of the spiritual life, everything ultimately leads us back to him. If I were a finger-wagger like my elementary school teachers, that's what I'd be doing right now. Jesus Christ is everything. "I am the way, and the truth, and the life," says Christ, "no one comes to the Father, but by me" (Jn 14:6). The whole point of the Christian life is to become like Jesus. He is our path to God. He is our salvation. We want to get back the likeness to God that Adam and Eve lost through original sin. "Prayer," says the *Catechism*, "restores man to God's likeness and enables him to share in the power of God's love [see Rom 8:16-21]" (2572).

Because Christ is the center, the Gospels are generally a good bet when it comes to preparing to converse with God in meditation. You can't love someone you don't know, and Scripture is the Word inspired (see 2 Tm 3:16). As St. Jerome famously declared, "Ignorance of the Scriptures is ignorance of Christ." Jesus actually modeled for us what it means to be perfect. Train your thoughts on him. Since he is not only saintly but sanctifying, it makes sense that the ordinary method of meditation centers on the life and words of Our Lord in Scripture.

At the risk of repeating myself, remember: meditation isn't rushing willy-nilly through whatever material we choose to meditate on. The spiritual life isn't a sprint. It's a marathon. Take your time. It's about soaking in the presence of God as in a hot tub after a long day of hard work.

As you prayerfully read and open yourself to the presence of God, he will begin to quietly speak to you. And this is an important point. In vocal prayer you're always the one talking. But in meditation, it's a conversation in which you must learn to listen, too. Sometimes God will talk to you about a certain area of your life which needs work. Other times he may bring to mind a person with whom you've been struggling to get along. Maybe you'll simply be overcome by how amazing he is and thank him in your heart for all the good he has done for you. Whatever God is showing or teaching, your main job is to respond. This is vital.

Just as cooking is not the same as eating, *methods* are not prayer. And when I say "methods," I'm referring to the different prayers or routines we get into during our time of meditation. Whatever we're doing, these are merely preparation. Technically speaking, recollection, reading, and reflection on divine things are not prayer. Rather, they show us what we should be seeking and present us with areas which require action. True meditative prayer consists in the movement of our heart and will to God. True prayer is "adoring, praising, thanking, and sorrowing with inner, quiet words," says the great spiritual writer Father Thomas Dubay. Prayer isn't process; it's relationship with a person.

Meditation is supposed to lead to interior action that affects your exterior behavior. That's the goal. Once your heart is moved toward God and the real conversation has begun, it's time to stop reading or reflecting. The method has done its job. Too often people get hung up on their method and lose the forest for the trees. We have to be ready to modify or even stop a particular method if it is no longer helping us talk with God. Be on guard against developing a routine and plowing through it no matter what. Prayer isn't about getting through your checklist of litanies and devotions. The goal is relationship with the person of Christ. And just as in any personal relationship, things change.

Think back to when you were dating. You didn't go to the same restaurant and movie every Friday or Saturday night, did you? ("Pizza and *Pretty in Pink* again? Of course, honey. I love Ducky.") No way! You were always thinking of something fresh, something new. (Tacos and *Top Gun*!) You wanted to do something that would lead to good conversation and growth in the relationship. It's the same with God.

On one hand, you don't want to stop doing a particular prayer routine because you're just not "feeling it." Remember, prayer isn't about emotion or feelings. On the other hand, if you're growing and your method or routine is no longer actively helping you engage God, dump it. ("Don't take it personally, Ms. Litany. It's me, not you.") Because the life of prayer is somewhat fluid, there may well be a time when you go back to some of these routines. ("We can still be friends. I'll call you later.") But if they're not useful right now, get rid of them. People who keep slogging through their method of choice no matter what will eventually wear out. Prayer will become a burden because they're not allowing the relationship to grow.

Pure and Simple

This danger is one of the reasons many spiritual greats encourage uncomplicated methods. Simple is generally better because grace is the prime mover of our prayer. We don't want to get in the way of the Holy Spirit. In fact, as time goes by and the Spirit works more and more deeply in our lives, the way we pray "naturally" begins to change. It actually gets simpler. There's "less" to it because the acts of faith, hope, and love brought on by our prayer finally fuse into an ardent love for God that doesn't require a lot of activity. The more docile we are to the Holy Spirit, the more our prayer becomes a prolonged spiritual communion instead of a series of steps we go through. God gives us grace, and we give him love.

The *Catechism* references a story of a peasant in Ars, France, whom St. John Vianney noticed coming daily to pray in front of the tabernacle. Upon being asked what he was doing the peasant stated, "I look at him and he looks at me"

(CCC 2715). This is the prayer of love, the prayer of simplicity — our methods of meditation prepare us for this. We're moving into a deeper relationship with Our Lord. We're at the point where we know each other so well that sometimes words get in the way. The prayer of simplicity indicates our transition to a new level of prayer — contemplation — that we'll discuss in the next chapter.

As we consider these different stages or kinds of prayer, it's important to bear in mind that they don't exist separately. In other words, you don't complete one type of prayer and move on to the next as you would a finished assignment. Growth in prayer is organic and gradual, not moving in only one direction. Even when you have advanced into the higher forms of prayer, there may be times when you dust off some old routine of meditative prayer because you feel the need to jump-start your interior life.

Of course, there are many reasons for the somewhat fluid nature of prayer. Chief among them might be you. It's impossible, for instance, to roll into an adoration chapel and slide into simplified prayer when you're habitually committing serious sin. Much of the way we pray is determined by how well we're living the spiritual life in general.

Greasing the Skids

Before we move on to a discussion of contemplative prayer, I want to make one final point about prayer in general, particularly meditation: it doesn't exist on its own. Prayer doesn't operate in a spiritual vacuum. It is ultimately tied to the sacraments, the "masterworks of God" which save us (CCC 1116).

As a Protestant, I grew up without the sacraments. Instead, the emphasis was on prayer, sermons on the Bible, and singing. (Potluck dinners receive an honorable mention.) Sacraments were not a part of my vocabulary. I viewed them as Catholic inventions. (Imagine my surprise when I read all about them in the early Church Fathers.) Some "high church" Protestants hold to some variation of sacramental theology (which still differs from Catholic teaching), but most of the forty-thousand-plus denominations did away with the sacraments a long time ago. It's a tragedy.

The sacraments are central to the Catholic faith because they are the ordinary means Christ uses to extend salvation to the world. In other words, they give us grace. Through the power of Christ they save us. And since they are our biggest channels of grace, everything we do is ultimately ordered to them, particularly the Eucharist. For this reason St. Irenaeus of Lyons declared back in the second century, "Our way of thinking is attuned to the Eucharist, and the Eucharist in turn confirms our way of thinking."[30]

Prayer prepares us for the sacraments. It paves the way for God's grace to have its maximum impact on our lives. There is enough grace in one consecrated Host to save the whole world. The only thing stopping it is us. Prayer gets "us" out of the way. It keeps the fire of love smoldering in our hearts so that when the wind of the Holy Spirit blows through the sacraments, the flame is ignited. We see this movement in Scripture.

Meditating on Emmaus

Hanging on the wall of many a Christian's home is the famous painting *Way to Emmaus* by Robert Zünd. It depicts the story from the Gospel of Luke in which Jesus joins two of his disciples on the road to the town of Emmaus on Easter Sunday (see 24:13-35). Without revealing his identity — they didn't recognize him — Jesus asks what they're discussing. They sadly recount that their hopes for liberation through Jesus of Nazareth, "a prophet mighty in deed and word," had been dashed by his crucifixion. And to confuse matters, earlier that very morning there had been reports of an empty tomb — no body was found.

After listening, Jesus chided them, "O foolish men … was it not necessary that the Christ should suffer these things and enter into his glory?" (vv. 25-26). He then began with Moses and the prophets and explained all that was in Scripture concerning him, the Christ.

Beginning to understand that Christ's sacrifice was for their eternal, spiritual salvation and not merely political liberation, the disciples excitedly asked if he would stick around for dinner. So he did. Celebrating the second Mass in the history of the Church (the first being the Last Supper), Jesus "took the bread and blessed and broke it, and gave it to them. And their eyes were opened and they recognized him; and he vanished out of their sight. They said to each other, 'Did not our hearts burn within us while he talked to us on the road, while he opened to us the Scriptures?'" (vv. 30-32).

What does this story have to do with prayer? A lot. The conversation between Jesus and these disciples was preparation for a celebration of the sacrament where an even deeper encounter with Christ occurred. This conversation is what we mimic in meditative prayer. Meditation is where we acquire Christ's spirit of love and sacrifice so we are more open to grace when we directly encounter his sacrificial love in the Mass. Prayer purifies our faith so that our spiritual eyes can be opened and the power of the Holy Spirit can move freely through the sacraments. The Spirit has to have room to work.

We can't underestimate the role of the Holy Spirit when it comes to prayer. Without him we couldn't converse with God. He is the grace poured into our souls which makes prayer work. Similar to his role as the love shared between Father and Son in the life of the Trinity, he moves us into union with God. Father Garrigou-Lagrange, the great Dominican theologian, says the breath of the Holy Spirit sustains our prayer and helps it go farther than it could based on its own virtues. And how far it goes is nothing short of incredible.

CHAPTER 8

Contemplation

Have you ever heard a little kid shouting, "Let me see, let me see!" as he pushed his way to the front of a crowd? Since the only thing my vertically challenged kids will ever dunk is a donut, one of them is often on my shoulders when anything interesting is happening. (I'm thinking of naming my next boy Zacchaeus.) Just being near the object of interest isn't enough. "I need to see, Daddy!" Ironically, their grubby hands often darken my own vision.

The other senses are certainly useful and great, but there is something about sight that helps us fully realize another's presence. Our kids need to "see" us watching when they perform. A boy and girl are "seeing" each other when dating. We go to "see" our relatives on vacation (again!). Seeing helps us to a deeper knowledge of the other person. "Where there is love, there is the eye," wrote Thomas Aquinas.[31] Contemplation, the third and highest stage of prayer, is the intimate sight and loving knowledge of God. It is the possession of his Presence, the only Presence that satisfies. "We wish to see Jesus" (Jn 12:21).

Practically speaking, contemplation is where things get a little hairy in a book about prayer. Why? Because this is very hard territory to describe. Even the great saints of prayer like John of the Cross and Teresa of Ávila struggled to provide a true glimpse of the highest levels of union with God. It is so otherworldly, so supernatural in origin that it's hard to fit into natural, human categories. But we're going to try anyway, because this is what we're after. Contemplation isn't just something reserved for saints. It's part of how we become saints.

Before attempting to define and discuss contemplative prayer, it's helpful to take a step back and restate a few key points. All prayer is ultimately directed to union with Christ. Prayer is a means. Its goal is God. But as with everything good, we can't achieve it without his grace, apart from which we "can do nothing" (Jn 15:5). This is especially true in contemplative prayer, where he is both the cause and the end, as we'll see. We have our part to play in preparing for it, but he alone can make it happen.

We need God's help because the final goal set before us is beyond comprehension. It is nothing short of becoming "partakers of the divine nature" of God (see 2 Pt 1:4). That's the gift he offers — a share in his divine life, full membership in his family. But for that to happen, we have to become like him, and we can't do that on our own.

I'm not talking about becoming more virtuous or getting to more Masses. That's certainly part of it. I'm talking about the whole enchilada; becoming like him because you've been "filled with all the fulness of God" (Eph 3:19). That's what begins to happen in contemplation. It's the consummation of our earthly spiritual life, the final plank in the bridge from time to eternity. God is made manifest in our very being — even if it doesn't seem so at first.

Slowly but Surely

Contemplation of God doesn't happen overnight. Like all the stages of prayer, it is typically a gradual process that unfolds over a lifetime. The different stages of contemplation — for there are several — are a growth of love. Often, people don't even realize they've begun the contemplative life. John of the Cross calls contemplation "a secret and peaceful and loving inflow of God."[32] It is a seed of transforming love quietly sprouting in the depths of the soul, moistened by the living waters of Christ himself. Given its mysterious nature, it's difficult to identify the movement from meditation into contemplation. But we're going to give it a shot.

Let's start by talking about what it is not. Because it's a more passive form of prayer, contemplative prayer differs from meditation. Meditative prayer consists of your actions, such as reading spiritual books, rubbing the varnish off rosary beads, and visualizing passages of Scripture. In other words, you're focusing your faculties on the mysteries of Christ. You're actively seeking out the truths of God. In contemplation you stop. John of the Cross says the difference between meditation and contemplation is "like that existing between toil and the enjoyment of the fruits of that toil; between the drudgery of the journey and the rest … at its end."[33]

Everyone knows that learning *about* something isn't the same as experiencing it. In meditation we learn what we need to do in order to unite ourselves to God, but the uniting still must take place. He must communicate himself to us in a real way that goes beyond our various (though necessary) spiritual pondering. That's what happens in contemplation.

While there are multiple levels of contemplation, generally speaking it is not something we initiate. (Some spiritual authors call the transition between meditation and contemplation "acquired contemplation," a form of prayer which still retains our initiative.) Infused contemplation, the entry into mystical prayer, is not something we can make happen. It's "an intimate sharing between friends" that comes from God.[34] It is a gift poured into us by God.

That doesn't mean we have no role in this spiritual drama. God's not going to give himself to just anyone. We have to demonstrate our desire for him. We must set the table for this great gift to be served. How do we do that? Primarily through meditation and doing our best to grow in virtue and holiness. We work at putting on our spiritual "Sunday best" every day in preparation for the arrival of the King. And we have to do it every day, because this is a process that takes time.

Slow growth is something a lot of people misunderstand or even try to get around. As twenty-first-century humans, we are accustomed to immediate gratification. As long as we have the cash, we can get pretty much whatever we want or need right away. But growth in the spiritual life and the art of prayer is not something that happens quickly. Any prayer "technique" that promises a quick and easy road to intimacy with God is simply false — especially if it involves campfires and multiple rounds of "Kumbaya." Just as transitions in the natural life are gradual as we move from infancy to adulthood, there aren't really hard markers in the spiritual life. It's not like you suddenly come to a posted sign during your prayers that declares: "Congratulations. You are now entering contemplation."

So how do you know you're there? As God begins to quietly pour himself into you in a new manner, you'll find indications of his presence in the way you live. That's the primary indicator. Lots of people think they'll be overwhelmed by emotion or incredible feelings when they achieve deep union with God. And, yes, it can and does happen. Bernini's famous sculpture *Ecstasy of St. Teresa* beautifully depicts how this great saint was enraptured and overwhelmed by the presence of God when she reached the highest levels of contemplation.[35] Her own description of the event tells how one of God's highest angels pierced her heart with a flaming dart, leaving her "all on fire with great love of God."[36] In another otherworldly experience she said: "It seemed my soul wanted to leave my body because it didn't fit there nor could it wait for so great a good.... The glory of this rapture was extraordinary."[37]

It might not be the initial or daily experience for everyone, but this "wonderful interior joy" described by Teresa and others shouldn't surprise us.[38] After all, we're talking about union with Almighty God. The Infinite taking hold of the finite. Ultimately, this is what we're made for. It's everything.

And yet we don't want to overemphasize experience or feelings, because this is a trap many fall into when analyzing the interior journey. We equate our mere human impulses with the voice of God, which often leads us astray. Consider yourself blessed if God rewards you with extraordinary experiences like that of Teresa and others. It's a great gift and foretaste of heaven. But the true litmus test of growth is how we're living, not our feelings — which tend to come and go faster than the taste of Fruit Stripe gum.

Even if we're receiving special graces — visions or "raptures" from Our Lord — spiritual union with God can't be separated from the day-to-day activities of our life. We are a union of body and soul. Spiritual growth must necessarily affect the way we act in the material world. When someone drops in out of nowhere at dinnertime and we don't freak, we're growing in prayer. When our child draws with permanent marker on the freshly painted wall and we don't scream words not even soap can wash out of our mouth, we're growing in prayer. If someone cuts us off in heavy traffic and we keep smiling with both hands on the wheel ... well, you get the idea. Growth in prayer is indicated by overall growth in virtue, a life lived more like Christ's. "You will know them by their fruits," says Our Lord (see Mt 7:16).

Humanity to Divinity

At this point you might be thinking: "Got it, Matt. It satisfies us like nothing else. It helps us live more like God. It can even lead to some pretty fantastic experiences. But I'm still in the dark here. Give me a solid definition of contemplative prayer." Fair enough. I don't know of a simpler one than this: contemplation is the manifestation of Jesus in your soul. It is the normal culmination of the life of prayer. "He who has my commandments and keeps them, he it is who loves me; and he who loves me will be loved by my Father, and I will love him and manifest myself to him" (Jn 14:21). If we're doing what we're supposed to do, contemplative prayer is the final preparation for heaven. It's the stage of our becoming consumed and filled up by God as we prepare for full union with him in heaven.

"Manifestation of Jesus in my soul, huh? That's still a bit nebulous. Can you feel it, Matt?" Maybe.

"Can you taste it?" Not sure.

"Can you smell it?" I'm starting to worry about you.

When trying to put a finger on contemplation you have to check your human notions at the door. We're dealing with the supernatural inflowing of the infinite God into our very finite being. It's like pouring the ocean into a thimble. That's why you don't find "cut and dried" definitions of this stage of prayer, even in the writings of masters like John of the Cross and Teresa of Ávila. Instead, they give us really "helpful" terms like "warmth" and "fragrance" to describe the phenomenon. (I guess you can smell it after all!) Not even their vast experience and knowledge can define it to our satisfaction.

The reason is that in a sense, as we move from meditation to contemplation, we're moving from humanity to divinity. We're moving from a human mode of praying to a supernatural communion. Meditation has sharpened our sight of God. The hours, months, and years spent in this stage of prayer have reordered our view of the world — we've placed Christ at the center and changed the way we live. But that's not the end. "We are meant to pass through the Sacred Humanity, to the Divinity which it veiled and clothed," says Father Leen.

As we have seen, the goal of prayer is participation in the divine life of God. That's the whole point of the Incarnation, death, and resurrection of Jesus. Joined to his life through the sacraments and prayer we become divine. We don't become one of the Trinity, mind you. We are never equal to God, though lots of people think they are. Rather, through his loving grace we become what he is by nature. He gives himself to us, his children. He grafts us into the Divine Family tree. In the life of prayer, this grafting is realized through contemplation.

"Whoa, Matt. This sounds like some pretty high-level stuff. Are you sure it isn't reserved for monks and nuns hanging out in monasteries and nunneries or whatever you call those places they live? Are you saying it's for the average Joe and Judy, too?" That's exactly what I'm saying. Yes, there are many levels of contemplation as we ascend to God, and certain vocations (might) provide more opportunity to climb to higher stages, but infused contemplation is for every Catholic. It's the natural end of our earthly prayer life, the final stepping stone to heaven, where we start getting close enough to "see," just like kids on my aching shoulders. Our limitless God begins to satisfy our eternal longings and fill our "capacity for the unlimited."[39]

Contemplation helps us to not only see God more clearly, but ourselves, too. We truly understand that the more we give ourselves to God, the more satisfied we'll be. This realization totally transforms a person's view of the "work" it takes to progress in prayer and the spiritual life in general. Before, we had to constantly fight against our desires for the bright, shiny objects that vied for our attention and distracted us. Even if we successfully shunned the baubles of this world, we still wanted them. But as we move into contemplative union with God, this changes. The things that keep us from him actually become unattractive.

Our joy at this point is in him alone. We're changing. Mysteriously, happiness and longing grow rapidly side by side. While our soul is "never at rest," says Father Leen, "it is never restless; though it is never satisfied it is never dissatisfied."[40] Why? Because we know we're moving toward that Person alone who can offer the intimate union for which we long. The inner thirst is being quenched bit by bit. But it's a paradox. The more he sates our hunger, the more it grows. For this reason

Paul exclaimed, "For to me to live is Christ, and to die is gain" (Phil 1:21). In other words, the further we travel toward God, the more we are satisfied, though our desire to fully arrive in his presence increases. It's kind of like vacation.

I hate the long car trips which accompany family vacation. I want to get from point A (home) to point B (the beach) as fast as possible. Forget detours to see the largest ball of twine on earth. My children are lucky if we stop for the bathroom. "You'll have to hold it, kids. We just passed the last rest stop on earth. Maybe we'll catch it on the way back."

Like other parents, my displeasure at vacation travel is somewhat related to the fact that I generally travel with a pack of half-tamed human children possessing bladders the size of a small marble. (Passing another rest stop is like playing chicken with a semi-truck. You have to be brave — or stupid.) I'm kidding, of course (kind of). I can't really blame their agitation. If I spent hours on end strapped in tighter than a launch-ready astronaut, I'd be a bit irritable, too. When I was a kid car seats were as much a reality as floating cars. If there were no regular seats left, parents put the youngest on their lap and let them steer. It was great driver's ed.

But even as I endure long travel as an adult I've noticed something. The longer the trip goes, the happier I become. I might have lost my mind along the way, but my desire to arrive at vacation paradise is slowly being satisfied the more miles I put behind me, even though I'm not yet there. The pain in my back now serves as a reminder I've already covered a lot of ground. The yelp of a child loses its power to annoy as I start to see signs for my exit. If the car breaks down now, we can simply leave it and walk the rest of the way. (Yeah, right!) I'm getting closer. I'm getting more relaxed. I'm good. But I still really, really want to get there; to lie on the sand listening to the crashing waves, hearing the seagulls, and smelling the salt in the air.

Your Presence Is Required

Alas, life isn't always a beach, but as we move toward union with God, the former pain we experienced seeking earthly satisfaction changes to longing. Pain turns to desire. While we're never fully satisfied here, the filling we do experience is a distinct pleasure because it's what we were made for. We know complete satisfaction is at hand. Even so, the gnawing hunger for God's full presence remains. We're seated at the table taking the first mouthwatering bite of the exquisite dinner for which we've been starving.

That being said, we must remember that, ultimately, satisfaction is not what we're striving for. We strive for God. That's why we keep going even when we don't feel like it — when our human frailties want us to stop or distractions abound. Rest assured, happiness and the fulfillment of all our desires is going to happen if we're seeking God. But it's not about us. It's about him.

Contemplation is a new relationship between the soul and God. He is being "realized" in us. This "realization" may come and go, especially in the initial stages of contemplation, but we have a new awareness of his presence. We are beginning that passage through his sacred humanity into his divinity. It's not natural. It's supernatural. It's from God.

At this point in our path to God, we're starting to love him for who he is, not for what he can do for us. We've even stopped focusing on virtues or habits, because we're focused on him. We don't have to think about them because the life of virtue is now naturally flowing into us from him. We receive it. We receive him. No longer do we have to move through created things to the Creator. In fact, meditative prayer often becomes drudgery to those who have achieved this stage of spiritual development.

Shortly after she became a postulant in the Order of the Visitation of Mary, Margaret Mary Alacoque, promoter of the Sacred Heart of Jesus devotion, got into trouble. She found it hard to meditate according to the order's rule. No matter how hard the poor girl tried, she couldn't concentrate on the material.[41] Little wonder, she was well into contemplation, receiving visions directly from Our Lord.

Be aware that there are times when to meditate would mean taking our eyes off the real manifestation of Christ. It's climbing back down the ladder, so to speak. Jesus is making himself directly known to us, so turning our vision to created things that merely point to him is pointless. If you find meditation hard because of a desire to simply be with Christ, set it aside and let God work.

Interestingly, many people get a little scared at this point. This kind of "passive" prayer where God is directly acting upon us is uncharted waters. What we're experiencing is amazing, but we're used to a particular path. In meditation it was much easier to see spiritual progress. Growth in virtue could be identified, and we could chart our development, so to speak. But not any longer.

When God gifts a soul with loving, passive prayer in contemplation, he takes over. He seizes the will. He's in control. We're no longer marking our own path toward him. For that reason, it's not unusual for anxiety to set in. Have we become lazy? Are we doing enough? The satisfaction of making our own way (aided by grace, of course) is gone. He's turned on the tractor beam and is drawing us to him. And while we don't exactly know what's happening, we really like it.

Transfigured

Father Leen uses the biblical story of the Transfiguration on Mount Tabor to illustrate what happens in this kind of contemplative prayer. During the years of his earthly ministry, Jesus' inner circle of Peter, James, and John achieved a high degree of intimacy with Our Lord. With him constantly, they were striving to imitate what they saw in his life. This human intimacy they achieved with Christ was, in a sense, their ordinary path of mental prayer, of meditation. But when he took them up the mountain and allowed his divinity to burst through the veil of his sacred humanity, they were "filled with awe" (Mt 17:6) as Jesus "shone like the sun" (Mt 17:2). Added to the light show was the appearance of Moses and Elijah — both of whom had been long dead. And if this weren't enough, they heard the very voice of God.

As a guy with a pretty low, Barry White-ish voice, I've noticed small children unaccustomed to my bass tones quiver in my presence if I get a bit loud. But can you imagine the biggest, baddest, subwooferest voice in the universe speaking to you? No wonder Jesus had to tell them to "rise, and have no fear" (Mt 17:7).

But the fear experienced by the disciples was not one of abject terror. Father Leen says "their fear was the bewilderment that the Human always experiences at contact with the Divine."[42] Not knowing what to do with himself, Peter blurts out, "Lord, it is well that we are here; if you wish, I will make three booths here, one for you and one for Moses and one for Elijah" (Mt 17:4). Poor Pete. In the delirium of their divine encounter he offers to make some tents. Overcome with the experience, Luke tells us, he didn't know what he was saying (9:33).

The three disciples were consumed with a desire to prolong this vision, this glimpse of Divinity. Who could blame them? They had received a prefiguration of the joy of heaven. The veil had been lifted ever so slightly, and they were overwhelmed, engulfed in the dazzling light and love of the Trinity. But, alas, even the disciples had to come back down the mountain and rejoin the rest of the world.

The Tabor experience is a great reminder that even upon reaching the heights of an encounter with God we're still tasked with the duties of this life. Cooking, cleaning, and diaper changing continue — forever, it seems. The difference, and it's a huge one, is that in this stage of union with God we have a sort of constant contentment and happiness because we're drawing ever closer to God. Our soul is constantly smiling, as it were, immersed in the joy of Our Lord. And don't forget that just because you might not experience intense supernatural delight (and least, not yet!), that doesn't mean you aren't encountering God in a deep way as you mature in the faith. Jesus was just as present with the disciples down in the valley as he was on Tabor. Contemplative prayer isn't an "over and done with" type of thing. It's an outpouring of God into our lives which enables us to live up to Paul's admonition to "pray constantly" (1 Thes 5:17).

Active Contemplation

Integrating the interior and exterior life is one of the hardest things to do. Most of us tend to be Martha, not Mary. Remember that story in the Gospel of Luke? Jesus is chilling out at Martha's place, and she's doing exactly what many of the rest of us would: running here, there, and everywhere trying to make sure everything is taken care of. (Can you imagine hosting the Son of God at your house?) Her sister Mary, on the other hand, is quietly seated at Jesus' feet, hanging on his every word. When Martha complains about how she's the only one working, Jesus gently rebukes her, saying: "Martha, Martha, you are anxious and troubled about many things; one thing is needful. Mary has chosen the good portion, which shall not be taken away from her" (Lk 10:41-42).

I confess I've got a soft spot for Martha. I probably would have piled on: "Yeah! Tell Mary to get to work." But Jesus is telling us first things come first, and he's it. It all starts with him. Yes, he offers us a part to play, but he doesn't need our help. We need his. He is the source of energy for all of our action.

The problem we often run into, especially in ministry situations where zeal is very present, is putting the cart before the horse. We're doers. We hear an idea we like and "bam!" we're on it. "Let's *do* this thing!" That's all well and good ... *if we're already engaged in a deep life of prayer*. Being an apostle doesn't mean just heading out to proclaim the Gospel in the hinterlands (which are really far away). We must first go "inside" and pack our spiritual bags before we can lead others on a journey to God. Living an active life without prayer is like taking an exam without ever studying or attending class. It's not going to end well.

We must remember all of our activity is based on love of God. It's all about leading others to him so he can save them and grant new life. Our activity needs to flow from the surplus of grace in our life. We fill up on Christ, and he overflows from us into others. That has to be the order, because we can't give what we haven't yet received.

The great Archbishop Fulton Sheen was the cat's meow of evangelization in America back in the middle of the twentieth century. A tireless promoter of the faith, he wrote over seventy books, led celebrities to conversion, and hosted radio and television shows for decades. He was so good he won a couple of Emmys for Most Outstanding Television Personality.

What made Fulton Sheen so great? He was a prayer warrior. He fueled up on Our Lord before spreading the fire of God's love. In fact, he made a decision early on that he would spend an hour a day in the presence of the Blessed Sacrament — in silence.

CHAPTER 9

The Sound of Silence

Have you ever noticed — or heard — that children like everything loud? Mine especially. The television has to be loud enough for the neighbors to enjoy our program. The music has to be loud enough for the previous owner of our home (sadly, deceased) to hear it. Their voices, though mere inches away, must always pummel my ear like a roundhouse from Sugar Ray Leonard. (I think we're related.)

I was the same way, of course. And when I was a kid it always drove me nuts that adults were constantly "shushing" me. Apparently it's hereditary. After being "shushed" several times during an especially long homily at Mass, my four-year-old son finally had enough. Pointing to the loquacious priest he loudly inquired, "How come Jesus gets to talk and I don't?"

While kids are particularly fond of the highest of decibels, the truth is few of us actually crave silence. We "shush" children so that we can hear something else we actually prefer, not silence. More often than not, we want to hear the radio, television, iPad, smartphone, another person — the list goes on and on.

In this day and age, we are conditioned for distraction and noise. It greets us at every turn. Images incessantly assault us. Music or chatter greets us at the grocery store, the mall, even the gas station. Noise constantly surrounds us, even when we aren't actively listening. You'd be hard-pressed to find an elevator not piping in a bad orchestral version of the Backstreet Boys or Bon Jovi. I was once even forced to endure "Muskrat Love" in an airport bathroom. (If that's not grounds for a lawsuit, I don't know what is.)

Why does society feel the need for constant diversion and noise? It's pretty simple, actually. Silence is scary. It makes us uncomfortable. Have you ever caught yourself getting annoyed or even anxious when technical or human error causes the dreaded "dead air" on the radio? You rush to change the station and breathe freely only after the silence has been broken. The pumping bass or the dulcet tones of yet another golden-throated deejay salve our angst and calm our spirits.

In silence we're confronted with ourselves. You could go so far as to say that silence puts us to the test. Free of distraction, it forces us to peer inside and be honest. I once read of a famous spiritual director who made anyone coming to see him spend an hour in an adoration chapel without any reading materials or other diversion. God did the heavy lifting for him.

Unfortunately, the modern world has no time or tolerance for silence. In a utilitarian universe obsessed with production and exploitation of resources, silence is of little value. How do you use it? What can you do with it? Who wants to pay for it? In the eyes of the world, silence is a "holy uselessness," says French philosopher Max Picard.[43]

One of our problems is a tendency to view silence as an absence of anything. But silence isn't a "nothing." Silence is the reality into which sound invades. It's always present underneath the noise. I love a line from Picard, who wrote, "Silence towers above all the puny world of noise; but as a living animal, not an extinct species, it lies in wait, and we can still see its broad back sinking ever deeper among the briers and bushes of the world of noise."[44] Loud though the world may be, we'll never be able to fully drown out silence. Like God, it had no beginning and has no end. "It is like uncreated, everlasting Being."[45]

And silence is sacred. That's why most people immediately lower their voices or stop speaking altogether when entering a beautiful church. The knowledge of who dwells there demands awe and reverence, which naturally translates into silence. Even the most beautiful piece of classical music is normally out of place in an adoration chapel. Silence is required to recollect ourselves and enter undistracted into God's presence. It's necessary to quiet the exterior noise that is always threatening to drown out our interior lives.

Silent Movies

From the moment I entered the dormitory my first year of college back in the eighties, I was amazed at the level of noise. In fact, one of the first scenes I witnessed in my new "home" was two freshman boys karate-fighting up and down my hallway while a yellow boombox blared the theme song "You're the Best" from *The Karate Kid*. It still gets me pumped up. Only now it's all about motivation for hand-to-hand combat with the laundry as opposed to fighting a fictional member of the Cobra Kai dojo.

While eighteen-year-old boys (one with a thin leather tie around his forehead) duking it out to loud music before classes even started is somewhat understandable, actually studying amid the cacophony of television shows or eighties arena rock always vexed me. Worse yet, students took pride in possessing the loudest stereo and were constantly seeking opportunities to prove it.

Not that I didn't enjoy turning The Outfield up to eleven every now and then, but the constant blare of loud music eventually becomes a battering ram knocking down the walls of sanity. I was once driven to physically threaten a hall mate who insisted on repeating The Eurythmics "Here Comes the Rain Again" as loud as his stereo could go for over twenty-four straight hours because he swore someone stole money from his room while that song was playing. He mistakenly believed it would drive the thief crazy enough to return the money. It turned out the thief lived in a different wing and didn't share my anguish over having a good song forever destroyed.

How in the world can a person even think in that kind of environment? I couldn't. That's why I almost had to resort to physical action. I couldn't take it anymore. My "sweet dreams" were not "made of this." It was a nightmare. Of course, trying to do your homework enveloped in noise is one thing. Trying to pray surrounded by noise and distraction is quite another.

We've already noted the importance of recollection when entering into prayer. Quiet is a necessity if we're going to put ourselves in the presence of God. "The Father spoke one Word, which was his Son," says John of the Cross, "and this Word he speaks always in eternal silence, and in silence must it be heard by the soul."[46]

But silence is something more than no sound. We must quiet our interior selves, too. If you haven't noticed, our minds love to wander all over the universe even when we're "quiet." Distraction from within is just as problematic as exterior disturbance. St. Teresa says to just laugh at distractions and give them back to God as part of prayer, but it's better if we're never distracted in the first place. That's why silence must be cultivated in every area of life. This doesn't mean you have to move into Maxwell Smart's "Cone of Silence" for the rest of your life. But it does mean reigning in your consumption of the world in general terms. Interior quiet isn't a switch you can flip (or a cone you can lower) any old time you want.

The sights and sounds we take in are food for the imagination. It's vitally important we guard what we allow to enter it. It's hard enough to focus when innocent distractions abound. It's downright impossible to move into the presence of God if your mind is picking through the trash you recently dumped in. Of course, it doesn't just stay inside. As the old saying goes: garbage in, garbage out.

Enough Said

The Letter of James in the New Testament scares me to death. It's the primary reason I took James as my confirmation name. He keeps me on the straight and narrow. Right from the get-go he's lobbing bombs in my direction. Even when I'm able to avoid the explosions, he still manages to get me, poking me in the eye with a verse like: "If anyone thinks he is religious, and does not bridle his tongue but deceives his heart, this man's religion is vain" (Jas 1:26). Never have I wanted someone so right to be so wrong.

As a participation in the divine life of God, our spiritual life is of a delicate nature. Even "small" venial sins (there's nothing actually small about any sin) can snuff out our fervor or derail our ascent to God. And there's no easier sin than saying something we shouldn't. Not controlling our tongue is one of the fastest ways to regress in the spiritual life.

One of the reasons James speaks so forcefully about our tongues is they're a great indicator of what's inside of us. "You brood of vipers! how can you speak good, when you are evil? For out of the abundance of the heart the mouth speaks" (Mt 12:34). Imperfections make themselves known in what we say. If we think lustful thoughts, it comes out in lewd speech. If we're envious of another person, we'll start to backstab. If we're angry, look out!

When we can actually tame the little monster in our mouth, it's a pretty fair indication we're practicing virtue in other areas of life. But since "the tongue is a fire ... full of deadly poison," this is all easier said than done (see Jas 3:6-8). History shows some people went to great lengths to avoid sins of the tongue. One of the reasons the Desert Fathers fled society was so they could stop talking. After all, it's kind of hard to speak poorly of people when there are none.

But what are the rest of us to do? Is everyone who lives in a city with more than a population of one in danger? The short answer is "yes." The long answer is, "Don't give up because there's hope." That's what grace is for.

Hush Up

Don't get the wrong idea about what I'm saying regarding the danger of speech. To talk is human. In fact, our ability to speak is one of humanity's distinguishing features. We use our tongues to communicate ideas, as well as to praise and pray to God. And, frankly, my total silence around the house would likely engender more than a few choice words from my wife. Even worse, she might stop talking herself — the dreaded "silent treatment."

God created the world through speech, and the Word of God was proclaimed verbally long before it was written down. The celebration of the liturgy needs words, too. Can you imagine a priest resorting to shadow puppets for his homily? Let's all take a moment and pray that never happens.

James says "bridle" your tongue, not cut it off (see Jas 1:26). We have to talk. If everyone stopped speaking, the unemployment lines would be full of mimes! (Hmmm. On second thought…) Rather than a total negation of speech, silence is a means to help us put our tongue to right use, something that remains a problem for most of us.

While it's obvious we must speak at appropriate times, it's more obvious that a lot of what we say should not be said. Much of our speech is motivated by pride, vanity, jealousy, anger, and a host of other bad things. How easily we slip into gossip when talking about another person. How delicious to thrust the knife of slander into someone's back. (A much better visual than backbiting.) For some reason we believe cutting someone else down to size will elevate our stature, while it only lowers our standing with God.

Even when not denigrating someone else, excessive talking can be problematic. Many of us love to chat. We desire to be the person with "breaking news" that others haven't yet heard. It gives us a sense of superiority and control that is nothing but selfish and egotistical. It's hard to escape this wicked satisfaction even when we're trying to help someone by providing new information or knowledge. Pride is a cruel taskmaster and rarely comes "in the name of love," regardless of what the band U2 sings.

Incorrect use of the tongue — and I don't mean licking a metal pole in winter — not only damages us but can easily cause others to fall, too. We love to set people up to get a response we desire. How simple it is to say something we know will elicit a negative comment from our companion. Even a question as innocuous as "Guess who called again?" is a problem when you know you're setting the other person up to roll his eyes and launch into sinful speech. Don't forget that Jesus said, "Temptations to sin are sure to come; but woe to him by whom they come!" (Lk 17:1).

Those are scary words. But they're not the scariest. If I had to pick one verse out of the Bible that always makes me shudder it would be Matthew 12:36. Jesus says, "I tell you, on the day of judgment men will render account for every careless word they utter." I don't know about you, but I've said some ridiculous things in my life for which I would much prefer to shake the eternal Etch-A-Sketch and start over. What are we supposed to do? How do we tame the beast? (Join me now in breast-beating.)

The solution is supremely simple, yet devastatingly difficult. Stop talking. Hush up as much as possible. Even when your emotions are running amok and you feel the need to lash out, think twice. In fact, think three times. Generally speaking, it's best to get control and put a sock in it. Oftentimes emotions lose their force if you don't express them. Mortify your tongue as you would your taste for chocolate or beer during Lent. Talking can lead to sinful satisfaction — deny yourself the opportunity. God gave us a tongue to glorify him.

Too often we simply glorify ourselves. As Mama always said, "If you can't say something good, don't say anything at all."

Of course, this is all pretty rich coming from a guy who makes his living in part by speaking to thousands of people every year. And it's a pretty solid bet that speech is necessary for the rest of you, too. But silence can be maintained even when speaking if we follow the "golden rule" of Father Leen:

> The rule is, never to speak merely for one's own sake or for one's own gratification, or to satisfy some impulse, but solely for the glory of God, for the right accomplishment of duty, for the promotion of truth, for the exercise of charity, for the comfort of the sorrowful and for the purpose of brightening the day of one's fellows.[47]

That's a lot to remember, so until I can, I'll probably just try to shut up. But note that silence isn't a virtue in and of itself. Otherwise, mimes would be the holiest people on earth. (Yes, I have a problem with mimes.) Silence becomes virtuous when it is intended to boost control over our interior lives. It's meant to help us gain command over our crazy imaginations and unpredictable feelings so we can grow. St. John of the Cross said: "What is most necessary for our advancement is to silence our appetites and our tongue. The language He [God] understands the best is the silence of love."[48]

True silence suffers, says St. Paul, when we are distracted from "whatever is true, whatever is honorable, whatever is just, whatever is pure, whatever is lovely, whatever is gracious … anything worthy of praise" (Phil 4:8). Essentially, silence is recollection applied to speech.[49] And it's a necessary habit if we're going to grow in Christ, who, after all, practiced this spirit of quietness.

Scripture says Jesus regularly escaped to the quiet of the wilderness to be alone with his Father (see Lk 5:16; 6:12). That's how important silence was to his deep life of prayer. And in the Gospel of Luke we read that he stayed up all night in prayer before choosing his apostles (6:12-13). In fact, prayer in solitude is how he kicked off his entire public ministry — the Holy Spirit "*drove* him out into the wilderness" after his baptism where he spent forty days and nights in solitude (Mk 1:12, emphasis mine).

So ask yourself: If the incarnate Second Person of the Most Holy Trinity needed to be quiet with God, doesn't it make sense we should, too? Enough said.

CHAPTER 10

How to Progress

Like most kids arriving at driver's education classes in high school, I was already convinced of my ability to navigate the busy streets of my neighborhood. These classes were simply a requirement, a rite of passage I must endure before I could cruise to the movies with my buddies. Hands on the wheel at ten and two? Please! How about right hand at six, left slung out the window waving to my people. That's how I roll — or so I thought.

When it came time to finally slide into the driver's seat of a car large enough to run over a small elephant without feeling a bump, I was ready. Who cared if I could barely see over the dashboard? Let's ride! I glanced across at the guy sitting next to me and briefly wondered why there was a second brake pedal installed on the passenger side of the car. I soon found out.

In retrospect, I'm surprised he didn't scream. Instead he channeled his terror into stomping the secondary pedal as hard as he could. Large moving pieces of colored metal flashed around us. Horns assaulted the suburban silence. I could smell death — or maybe it was just exhaust. Regardless, cars were coming from everywhere, swerving at breakneck speed with drivers hurling expletives my way. (I would've shrunk down, but I could barely see to the end of the hood as it was.) We stopped, hard. The gym teacher/driver's education instructor grabbed the wheel. I don't remember exactly what he said, but it was forceful. Somehow between my feet on the gas, his on the secondary brake, and four hands on the wheel, we escaped. In the end, the only things damaged were my pride and his blood pressure.

In truth, it wasn't really fair. This particular intersection to which he subjected me is affectionately known to locals as "Suicide Circle." It's where six streets come together in one of those circular deathtraps some city planner mistakenly thought to be a bright idea. ("On this chart you can see where we'll have dozens of cars converging from multiple directions, merging, and seamlessly peeling off into different streets. Any questions?") The whole event shook me ever so slightly. Regardless, I take solace in thinking that perhaps, after a stiff drink or two in the teacher's lounge, my instructor realized that Suicide Circle plus Chicago rush hour plus new teenage driver didn't equal his best idea.

In addition to personal cathartic benefits, the point of telling you this story is that while I possessed the will to drive, I still needed to master the art of moving the machine in the right direction. All those pedals, mirrors, and steering wheel were meant to work a particular way which required knowledge and skill. I could name all the parts of the car and describe their function before I had any training, but I needed to develop some new traits and habits before cruising to the mall. Prayer works the same way. There are certain things we must master or we're not going to progress.

Persevere

The most important rule of prayer is to never stop. St. Paul exhorts us to "pray constantly" (1 Thes 5:17). Jesus agrees, declaring we "ought always to pray and not lose heart" (Lk 18:1). And to drive the point home, he tells a parable about a widow who kept bugging a godless judge over and over to rule in her favor in a dispute. At first the judge refused, but eventually she drove him nuts and he caved just to get her off of his back. "Though I neither fear God nor regard man …

I will vindicate her, or she will wear me out by her continual coming" (Lk 18:4-5). So if this unrighteous judge gave in, says Jesus, "will not God vindicate his elect, who cry to him day and night? ... I tell you, he will vindicate them speedily" (Lk 18:7-8).

To make sure we get the message, Jesus tells another story — that of the buggiest friend in the world. This guy has the nerve to bang on his buddy's door asking for bread at midnight. Jesus says the friend in bed won't give him the bread because of their friendship, but rather because of the door-banger's annoying persistence.

The moral of these parables isn't to glorify being a pain in the keister. Rather, Jesus is basically repeating the truism that the squeaky wheel gets the grease. "Ask, and it will be given you; seek, and you will find; knock, and it will be opened to you" (Lk 11:9).

As a parent, I'm starting to think that all children hear these stories right before they're born. I can see it now. God cracks open the Bible and tells the babies, "Okay, let me show you how this works..." As soon as the pale, sterile glow of hospital lighting illuminates their scrunched up little faces, they've mastered the art of perseverance. It starts with the cute cry of a newborn, but eventually morphs into wails of "Can I have this? Can I have that? I want more..." They ask over and over and over until you just can't take it anymore. Oh, the humanity! "Yes! You may have another Popsicle. Take the box. Take the whole refrigerator! In fact, here are my keys. I know you're only five years old and three years old. One of you push the pedals and the other steer; you're fast learners."

Okay, maybe I don't let them drive, but sometimes we give in because we've been worn down like the knees on an old pair of corduroy pants. But God gives in purely because of love.

Perseverance has to be based on faith and love. If we don't ever think there's a possibility it will happen, we wouldn't even ask. Regardless of my bluster, my children had to know there was at least a small chance that eventually I would cave in and get a dog. It's the same with God. But unlike me, the question isn't whether or not God will come through. He always does. The question Jesus asks at the end of the story of the persistent widow is the only unanswered part: "when the Son of man comes, will he find faith on earth?" (Lk 18:8). Believe in the goodness of God and trust him to answer your (persistent) prayers. But that's not all.

Don't forget that when the request is granted, we have to make full and right use of what we get so that the grace given isn't wasted. If my daughter, for example, begs me to let her stay up past bedtime because she has an assignment due, I'm willing to allow it. But if I were to catch her playing games on the computer instead of finishing her work, I'm far less inclined to say "yes" the next time she asks. Use the gifts God gives the right way and he'll continue to respond, which should lead us to humble thanks.

Humility

Humanity loves pride. We're proud of it. We glorify it. Like peacocks we flaunt beauty, intelligence, physical prowess, and anything else we can show off. We want to be recognized, and creating a name for ourselves is a life's ambition. Some of us even dream of being as big as God. Early in her career, pop singer Madonna reputedly said, "I won't be happy until I'm as famous as God."[50]

At one point, The Beatles actually thought they were. Back in the sixties John Lennon (now deceased) famously stated, "We're more popular than Jesus." (Can you imagine that conversation at the pearly gates?)

Pride is nothing new to the story, of course. Way back in the beginning of history Adam and Eve wanted to be as big as God, too, and got booted out of Eden as a result. Satan fell to the same temptation before Adam and Eve did and had to exit heaven. Later in human history the guys building the Tower of Babel wanted it to reach heaven in yet another failed effort to make a name for themselves. It's an old story that keeps repeating itself because of sin. In fact, pride is the source of sin. And there's only one way to kick it out: humility.

If pride is the root of sin, humility is the taproot of all the virtues. It feeds the virtues so that pride can be crushed. Pride is dangerous because it basically says that we have all the answers and we're in control, not God. That's why pride kills prayer. What's the point of asking God for anything if you think you can get it yourself? Spiritual writers often emphasize the importance for beginners in the spiritual life of meditating on the fact that we are nothing. This kind of mental prayer crushes pride because it puts us in our proper place and leads to gratitude.

The humble man recognizes he is merely a creature. He knows he has no existence apart from God and happily gives himself to God's will. Ultimately, that's what the Christian life is all about, which is why the *Catechism* calls humility the "foundation of prayer" (2559). In fact, humility is so important it led St. John Chrysostom to declare that the combination of humility and sin is better than a mixture of virtue and pride. To prove his point, he invites us to consider Jesus' parable of the Pharisee and the publican in Luke chapter eighteen:

> One relied on his righteousness, on his own fasting and the tithes that he paid. The other needed to say only a few words to be free of all his sins. That was because God was not only listening to his words, he also saw the soul of him who spoke them, and finding it humble and contrite he judged him worthy of his compassion and love.[51]

Jesus closes the parable by saying, "I tell you, this man went down to his house justified rather than the other; for every one who exalts himself will be humbled, but he who humbles himself will be exalted" (Lk 18:9-14). And Jesus didn't just tell us. He showed us. I don't know of a more striking passage in Scripture than this:

> Christ Jesus ... though he was in the form of God, did not count equality with God a thing to be grasped, but emptied himself, taking the form of a servant, being born in the likeness of men. And being found in human form he humbled himself and became obedient unto death, even death on a cross. (Phil 2:5-8)

Think about that. Jesus Christ, the Second Person of the Most Holy Trinity, the eternal Son of God, became like one of us, his creatures. Christ's becoming man, his incarnation, is an amazing act of love though difficult to understand. Jesus' humility led him not just to become like one of us, but to present himself to be beaten, spit upon, cursed, and finally crucified by his own creations. It's a gift of self we can barely begin to grasp. "God's positive hunger for humiliation, degradation, ignominy, is incomprehensible to our human understanding," said Archabbot Benedict Baur.[52]

Christ's life is a prayer, an offering of self back to the Father. He shows us the way. And if right now you're thinking, "Not only is this humility thing hard, look where it got Jesus. They killed him!" — don't forget to keep reading. The very next verse says that as a result of his humility and obedience, "God has highly exalted him and bestowed on him the name which is above every name" (Phil 2:9). None of us, not you, not me, not The Beatles, and certainly not Madonna, will be exalted over Christ. But living a truly humble life makes us like him, which is our aim. Humility clothes us with Christ. It's the "ornament of the godhead," says Isaac of Nineveh.[53]

Humility enables us to enter into a relationship with Jesus and participate in his divine life. It provides a direct line to God. As the Book of Sirach says, "The prayer of the humble pierces the clouds" (35:17).

In short, you can't ascend to heaven and commune with God unless you humbly lower yourself before God and men. Nothing kills the spiritual life faster than pride. Indeed, "pride goes before destruction" (Prv 16:18). It brought Adam down, and it will bring you down too, if you let it. That's why St. Teresa of Ávila exhorted us to "have humility and again humility! It is by humility that the Lord allows Himself to be conquered so that He will do all we ask of Him."[54]

Suffering

As time goes by and our spiritual aptitude increases, prayer stops being something we simply check off our Catholic to-do list. It becomes a constant awareness of God's presence in our life leading us to become more and more like him. It's a perpetual movement affecting all our decisions. We begin to see Christ in every person and situation — even challenging ones.

People serious about growing closer to God know they are going to come face-to-face with the issue of suffering. They're not the only ones, of course. As we've seen, everyone has to deal with suffering in some way, shape, or form, because we all experience it.

The big difference between Catholics and everyone else is how we view and handle the pain of this life. Joined to Christ through the sacraments, beginning with baptism, we have the opportunity to offer up our sufferings in union with Jesus. It's a tremendous grace. Jesus, the "last Adam," according to Paul, took the awful consequences of the first Adam's fall — suffering and death — and made them the path of life (see 1 Cor 15:45). In other words, Jesus flipped the devil's plan upside down. Satan thought he'd won. Man had turned against God and reaped the consequences. But Jesus said, "Not so fast." Out of humility and love, and like us in every way except sin, he experienced suffering and death and made them the path to salvation (see Heb 4:15). In fact, he became human for the express purpose of suffering and dying. He knows exactly what being human feels like in every respect (minus sin). Don't think God can't identify with your situation.

Christ's actions have changed everything. Now, whenever we experience difficulty of any sort, simply by saying, "Jesus, I offer this suffering up to you," we become an instrument of grace for ourselves and others. He gives us the power to help out the rest of his Body, our family members. For this reason St. Paul exclaimed, "Now I rejoice in my sufferings for your sake, and in my flesh I complete what is lacking in Christ's afflictions for the sake of his body, that is, the Church" (Col 1:24).

Because Christ wills it, we have the opportunity to participate in his work of redemption. He could do it all by himself if he chose, but he wants us to work with him. When we suffer and offer it to God, we're acting just like Jesus Christ. This is the path to eternal life. "United with him in a death like his, we shall certainly be united with him in a resurrection like his" (Rom 6:5). Jesus himself said, "If any man would come after me, let him deny himself and take up his cross daily and follow me" (Lk 9:23).

This is part of the beauty of our faith. Something we're going to have to deal with one way or the other becomes a powerful weapon in our spiritual struggle. And the more you practice offering your suffering back to Christ, the more suffering begins to take on a new dimension.

As we saw while discussing the Illuminative and Unitive Ways, suffering loses its bite as we mature in the spiritual life. Not only do we come to a deeper awareness that our suffering can help others; we know we're becoming more conformed to Our Lord.

"Got it, Matt. Suffering makes me more like Christ. I'm still working on exactly how I'm not going to mind it so

much, but I'll take your word for it. Let's move on. Shall we?"
Not just yet, my faithful reader. There's one more aspect of
suffering we need to discuss: its connection to prayer.

Working It Out

You can't separate suffering and prayer. They go together like
peanut butter and jelly, Abbot and Costello, or even Hall &
Oates (though I wish they'd broken up earlier). This is evident
in a couple of ways. First, as we said, prayer helps us to see
Christ in all situations, even those in which we suffer (which
might involve listening to Hall & Oates). It prepares us to accept God's will in everything. But there's another side of it, too.

Through prayer we begin to recognize various faults
and shortcomings in our lives. This happens particularly in
meditation when God points out areas that need work, as
discussed previously. But as any kid who watched GI Joe on
TV learned, "Knowing is only half the battle." We have to
do something about it. That's where the suffering comes in,
especially in the form of penance.

Penance is like a workout for your spiritual body. A
good friend of mine likens penance to the process of losing
weight. Early in life you're young and svelte. But then you hit
middle age and suddenly around your middle there appears a
spare tire. (They don't call the wheel in your trunk a "donut"
for nothing.) So what do you do? Well, either you reach for
another piece of cake, or you squash your desire for food and
stop eating as much. You suffer a little. You go hungry. You
work out. Why? In order to get stronger and healthier. It's the
same with our spiritual life.

Just as in physical workouts, penance and suffering
play a part in spiritual conditioning. They purge us of vices
and faults. But purging isn't enough. Once we get rid of our
spiritual "dead weight," we need to replace it with something
better, some spiritual muscle. Saints and other spiritual writ-

ers talk a good bit about replacing our vices with virtue. That should be our prayer request so that we don't fall back into sin. We can't just spiritually fast; we have to work out, too. But even that is just part of the process.

Detachment

Unless you're a masochist, penance is not an end. It's a means. The goal of penance is detachment from the things of this world. In particular, it's getting rid of anything which spiritually drags us down or keeps us from fixing our eyes on heaven.

The name of the game in the spiritual life is gaining control over ourselves. It's paramount because as St. John Paul II said, we must fully possess ourselves before we can give ourselves away.[55] It took me a long time to really grasp what the pope was saying in that statement. My grad-school roommate casually tossed it out in conversation one day after he'd learned it in one of his philosophy classes. I turned it over in my head quite a bit and finally concluded it's one of the most profound thoughts I've ever encountered.

John Paul II was basically saying we can't give away what we don't own. Imagine if a friend walked into your house, grabbed your nicest piece of furniture and gave it to another buddy. What would you do? (Yeah — me, too.) The pope applied this idea to the deepest parts of the person.

If we're ruled by our passions and desires, we're not in the driver's seat. We're not in control of our own selves. We're relegated to the back like a toddler strapped into a car seat with no choice over where the vehicle travels (except when they scream). That has to change. Otherwise, we can't make a gift of ourselves to others and to God. That's the role of penance. It strengthens our ability to control our actions and not be ruled by our passions. We can put the cookie down and slowly back away. We can control our anger when someone wrongs us. We can turn the channel when the show gets steamy. In short, penance helps us detach ourselves from this world.

These days "detachment" carries some negative connotations. Unless you're intent on maintaining your bachelor status, no guy wants to be labeled as "detached." "Detachment parenting" would probably land you in jail (unless you're dealing with your thirty-year-old who won't leave the house). Not even a retina wants to be detached. Regardless, it's an idea frequently discussed by the spiritual giants of our faith.

We want to be crystal clear about this because some people totally misunderstand spiritual writers like St. John of the Cross and St. Francis de Sales on this point. They think detachment essentially means we're supposed to be robots; not loving, not happy, not sad — not human! That's not it at all. As a parent, I'm attached to my kids. As a son, I'm attached to my parents. As a music lover, I'm totally attached to the eighties. There's lots to love in this world (and not love — like Hall & Oates).

It's not that we're to be cold or indifferent to anyone and anything. On the contrary, in the beginning God created everything good. We just need to remember that as good as creation is, it's not the Creator. When human attachments begin to impede our journey toward Christ, there's a problem. We can't allow ourselves to become so fixated or closely attached that we can't let go. (Even 38 Special knew to "hold on loosely.") And this is true of everything and everyone. Christ must be first. And this can be very difficult at times.

My family was not particularly pleased when I announced I was going to become Catholic. I don't blame them. Most of them are strong Christians with deeply held beliefs, and they simply didn't agree with what I was doing. But as much as I love them, I couldn't let that love impede my move into the Church. Jesus said, "He who loves father or mother more than me is not worthy of me" (Mt 10:37). I assure you it wasn't easy, and suffering occurred on both sides. But I think they realized on some level I was trying my best to follow where God was leading. And that's the point.

Detachment from this world doesn't mean we forsake it. I still love my family very much and enjoy visiting them when possible (except when I have to sleep on a couch). God made me a part of that family. He gave us the good of this world for our enjoyment. But we have to make sure our priorities are right. Otherwise, declare the saints, we're in trouble.

In his classic work *The Ascent of Mount Carmel*, John of the Cross discusses how we become slaves to things we love. While true love creates equality between persons as they seek to serve each other, disordered love creates slavery to sin. It rules our lives and subjects us to its power. Attachment to this world leads to worldliness, "for love effects a likeness between the lover and the loved."[56] The goal is to become "otherworldly," like Christ, not his creatures.

CHAPTER 11

To Whom Do We Pray?

Catholics love to pray. Our Fathers at Mass. Hail Marys at football games. "Bless us, O Lord" over meals. We even pray before the 50/50 raffle and silent auction at the Catholic school fundraiser. ("Please God, I need that autographed helmet for my wet bar. Please!") We're always praying.

Normally, our prayers are directed to the Father. After all, that's how Jesus told us to pray. Needless to say, we also pray to the other members of the Trinity. By its very nature, Christian prayer is Christ-centered. It is through the power of the name of Jesus that we have the ability to reach the Father. But this wasn't always the state of affairs.

Back in the Old Testament, people weren't allowed to utter the divine name of God. To this day, many Jews still refrain from using it, writing his name as "G-d" (which I've always had trouble pronouncing). For Christians, though, this all changed with the Incarnation of the Son. By assuming our humanity, he became our conduit back to the Father, a connection that had been disrupted by sin. Through the power of the Holy Spirit, we now have the ability to call upon the name of the Lord. He is our lifeline. For "there is one mediator between God and men, the man Christ Jesus" (1 Tm 2:5).

Unfortunately, the accusation often hurled at Catholics is that we go directly against this verse when we pray to the saints. Obviously, we strongly disagree, though this wasn't always the case for me personally. Don't tell anyone, but I had a hard time with some devotions and prayers to saints even after I'd been Catholic a few years.

Inside, Outside, Upside Down

In my former life as a real estate developer I once worked with an agent who buried statues of St. Joseph in the back yard of every house she listed. She wasn't a particularly devout Catholic from what I could tell, but she swore by her method. It drove me nuts. Seriously, how could anyone believe that burying a three-inch plastic statue would facilitate a house's sale? It smacked of idolatry. Plus, didn't it occur to people that St. Joseph had better things to do?

So when I accepted a job in a different state there was never any question as to how I was going to sell my house. No statues. No incantations. No superstition. Aggressive marketing, correct pricing, and great staging would get it done. After all, I felt certain this job change was the Lord's will, and God helps those who help themselves, right? So I started the brutal task of preparing my house to sell: cleaning, repairing, and the worst part — painting. Fortunately, I only had to repaint the walls from three feet down since my small children could only graze the house like deer through a forest.

To exacerbate my dilemma, I was attempting to sell my house when the real estate market crashed. It was so bad in our area that one of my friends had been trying to sell his house for almost three years with no luck. I needed to sell mine in six weeks! So I got to work.

For several weeks my family endured the misery of open houses and private showings to no avail. Everyone who has experienced this purgation knows it's exhausting. The house has to remain immaculate, which means you start following your children around with a vacuum cleaner and a sponge, muttering diabolical threats. You're constantly cleaning the bathroom, dusting the furniture, and you can't even throw your socks on the floor! The only plus is that you get to eat all the cookies you're supposed to bake in order to make your house smell better. We did everything we were supposed to do, but we didn't receive even a single offer. Desperation began to set in and pressure began to mount as time started to run out. We couldn't afford to have two mortgages. This house had to sell!

I'm not sure what first brought it to mind, but somehow those little statues of St. Joseph began to fill my thoughts. Maybe it was the fact that the town in which I lived was actually named St. Joseph. (I'm quick that way.) Regardless, I decided that desperate times called for desperate measures. Throwing theological caution to the wind I decided to buy a statue. To my chagrin, I had to drive thirty minutes to a Catholic bookstore at Notre Dame to even find one. (One of life's greatest unsolved mysteries remains the fact that you can't purchase a statue of St. Joseph in the town of St. Joseph.) It cost me gas and time, but it wasn't a total loss, I reasoned. At least my reputation — whatever it was — would remain intact if I bought one out of town. I didn't want my friends to know what I was doing.

Cautiously walking through the door of the bookstore I paused, looking to my left and right. The sales clerk took one look at me and said, "You're looking for a St. Joseph statue, aren't you?" I was stunned. How could she know? Bewildered, I nodded, and she pointed to a shelf lined with the most kitschy-looking Catholic paraphernalia I had ever seen. And that's saying something. It was an actual St. Joseph real estate sales kit, replete with the feared three-inch statue and instruction book. I had sunk to a new low. I bought the kit and rolled.

Begging God for forgiveness in case I was sinning — just as I did when praying my first Rosary, come to think of it — I buried the statue in my garden. The next evening a couple of friends came over to hang out. One of them, a priest, was my spiritual director. The other was a Protestant who was moving toward Catholicism. As he walked into my backyard, my Protestant buddy playfully asked where my St. Joseph statue was located. To his shock, I sheepishly pointed to my garden. My spiritual director couldn't believe it either. "C'mon, Matt! I'm trying to get people to stop doing that," he chided. I changed the conversation quickly and served drinks, always a good diversion.

The next day I stood out in the backyard and decided I had better dig it up. I didn't want to offend God, and the words of my very holy and wonderful spiritual director were ringing in my ears. I reached down into the soil and unearthed St. Joe. Even as the dirt fell from his tiny, plastic body, the phone rang. Somebody wanted to see the house! But here was my dilemma. I had just dug him up. The dirt was still fresh. Was he supposed to be buried or not? It was a serious quandary!

After a moment or two of angst, I took him inside, washed him off, and put him on the mantle. To my strong dismay, the people who came to see the house decided they didn't want it. "That's it!" I declared. Grabbing St. Joseph, I went back to the garden and buried him following the exact directions of my kit; upside down and facing my house. I didn't want my neighbor's house to sell, after all. It wasn't even on the market. Imagine their surprise.

After the deed was done, I prayed: "God, I know there's no power in this statue. This isn't an act of superstition. It's simply a humble act of piety. I'm asking for St. Joseph's help the same way you did as a child." Two days later I had a contract on the house for twenty thousand dollars more than expected, signing papers the day I moved.

Heavenly Prayers

I'm sure you have a great story of a saint's intercession in your life. Most Catholics do. That's because the *Catechism* tells us the saints "constantly care for those whom they have left on earth" (2683). They do this because we are all part of the same family. The saints in heaven are basically our older brothers and sisters who have "been there and done that." They know how to pray for us better than anyone else. For this reason, the Church encourages us to "ask them to intercede for us and for the whole world" (CCC 2683). But what about that pesky verse in the First Letter of Timothy where Paul says Jesus is the only mediator between God and man?

Allow me to answer the question with another question. When you're dealing with a big issue in your life, don't you often ask other people to pray for you? Of course you do! The Bible flat out says we should (see Jas 5:16; Eph 6:18; 1 Tm 2:1). In 1 Timothy 2:5, Paul is identifying the unique role of Jesus. As fully God and fully man, the Incarnate Word of God is the bridge between us and God. Everything ultimately goes through him. But don't forget that we have all "put on Christ" through baptism (Gal 3:27). We're family, incorporated into his Mystical Body. Asking prayers of those who have gone before us, our older siblings, is as natural as me asking you.

Of course, some people don't believe the saints in heaven can hear our prayers, that somehow they're cut off from the rest of the world. But that's certainly not what the Bible indicates. For example, Revelation says the saints in heaven are lifting up our prayers to God, interceding for us by offering "golden bowls full of incense, which are the prayers of the saints" (Rv 5:8), So, praying for those remaining on earth is one of the jobs of those in heaven. They're interceding for us.

Part of the problem for those who lack this understanding is the notion that once in heaven prayer stops because it's no longer necessary. This is mistaken and doesn't jibe with the apostle John's vision of heaven in Revelation. And Scripture tells us that even God prays. Jesus, who even on earth always remained the Second Person of the Trinity, was constantly in prayer with his Father. Once in heaven, the Letter to the Hebrews says, he "lives to make intercession" for us (7:25). Prayer doesn't stop once we're in heaven. It gets more intense! St. Paul says the Holy Spirit "intercedes for us with sighs too deep for words" (Rom 8:26).

Come, Holy Ghost

Let's take a moment to talk about the Holy Spirit. As in so many other three-person groups, he's often the forgotten member. (Raise your hand if you can remember the poor guy left sitting on the mother ship when Neil Armstrong and Buzz Aldrin played golf on the moon and posed for that MTV promo. Anyone? Bueller?)

I think we have trouble remembering the Holy Spirit partly because he's hard to visualize. There's the Father (old, long white hair, and thick beard), the Son (seventies-style shoulder-length locks and kindly face), and the Holy Spirit (uhhhhh ... some kind of a ghost?). It's hard to picture the Spirit that proceeds from the Father and the Son. How do you envision the love shared between them and given to us?

As hard as he is to picture, we have to remember the only way we can even say "Jesus is Lord" is through the power of the Spirit (CCC 2670; 1 Cor 12:3). It's the Spirit that gives us the grace to pray in the first place. It's the Spirit through whom we are "divinized" at baptism, receiving adoption as true children of God's family (CCC 1988). It is the Spirit that cleanses us from our sins and communicates to us "'the righteousness of God through faith in Jesus Christ'" (CCC 1987; Rom 3:22).

People may pray in all kinds of ways and languages, but it is all done through the power of the Holy Spirit, the "artisan" and "Master of Christian prayer" (CCC 2672). He is Christ's gift to us. But he doesn't just unite us to our Brother. The Holy Spirit draws us to our mother, too.

Mary

St. Louis de Montfort famously declared, "He who has not Mary for his Mother has not God for his Father."[57] I admit it took me a long, long time to come to grips with this view of Mary. I'm certainly not the only convert to struggle with Mary. Lots of us have. But can you blame us? Most of us were indoctrinated against her from the beginning. And if we weren't actively taught to regard Catholic belief about her as idolatry, she still played a very, very — and I mean *very* — small role in our Protestant past. The only time we ever talked about her was at Christmas.

Looking back, it's pretty funny that we put statues of Mary in our crèches for our plays and pageants. Paying this much attention to her would have been an act of idolatry any other time of the year. (Of course, I use the term "statues" loosely since they're generally plastic figurines illuminated by a light bulb.)

Regardless, my Catholic understanding of Mary took shape through the idea of family. I wrestled through all the other theological and scriptural arguments with regard to Our Lady, but it was through fully "getting" the whole family motif of God that I finally "got" Mary.

Since I am joined to Christ through the sacraments, God is really my Father and Jesus is truly my brother. Through the power of the Holy Spirit I'm joined to the Trinity and to all other members of the Body of Christ. That's a lot of people. But there's someone missing. What kind of a family doesn't have a mother?

The Reader's Digest Condensed understanding of Mary's divine maternity is this: Mary is the mother of Jesus. Jesus is God. Therefore, Mary is the Mother of God (*Theotokos* in Greek). It's that simple.

Jesus is one divine Person, both fully God and fully man. You can't separate out his humanity from his divinity like the marshmallows from the oats in Lucky Charms. His humanity isn't an outfit draped over his divine body, something he takes off before going to bed at night. He joined his human nature to his divine nature forever at the Incarnation in what's technically called the "hypostatic union" (not to be confused with what happens to your socks coming out of the dryer). His two natures are "united in the one person of God's Son" (CCC 481). And since Mary is the Mother of God, and we're members of the Body of Christ, she's our mother, too. That's why she plays a special role in our life of prayer. She's the one woman chosen from among all the billions ever born to be the mother of us all.

I used to think that Catholics were making up this whole Mary thing, an extra ingredient tossed into the salvation salad for some reason. But she's no extra. God is the origin of the pattern of our redemption. The template is his. He gave Jesus to us through Mary, and she works to give us back to him. St. Augustine declared, "All the elect are, in this world, hidden in the womb of the Most Blessed Virgin, where they are cherished and nourished and fostered and reared by this good Mother until such time as she brings them forth to glory after their death."[58]

Contrary to what I was taught growing up, she isn't somehow a fourth member of the Trinity. She's not the "one mediator between God and man." Rather, through his power alone, she is God's instrument of grace. And in our work and prayers, we need to use the same instruments of grace God does. Mary is the most finely tuned, most perfectly pitched of those instruments. So dust off your rosaries, fire up your Memorares, and proclaim your litanies to Our Lady. The same mama who taught the Son of God to pray, is ready to teach and guide us, too — now, "and at the hour of our death."

Prayers for the Dead

Sitting in front of a rose bush in my backyard is a pretty statue of St. Thérèse of Lisieux. She's one of my family's favorite saints. My oldest daughter took the Little Flower as her confirmation saint, and "Therese" graces the names of several girls in my family. Providentially, as I pen these words, the Church is celebrating her feast day.

Interestingly, the statue in my yard didn't come from a Catholic. It came from my mom. In the last few years of her life, my mother somehow developed a strong devotion to Thérèse. And I mean strong. She made a pilgrimage to Lisieux and even wrote a children's book about her. Still Protestant, I considered all of this quite strange. My dad was an ordained Protestant minister, for crying out loud. I vividly remember when he and my mom placed the statue in the yard of my childhood home. Being a good little Reformer, I was more than a bit embarrassed and no doubt spent time devising how I would explain it to my friends. ("Yeah, dude ... some hardcore Catholic punks vandalized our yard last night with a saint! Can you believe those jerks?")

These days I couldn't be happier about that statue. Every time it catches my eye I think of my mom. And often, these thoughts lead to prayers for the repose of her soul. I find these prayers one of the most comforting facets of our faith.

Catholic teaching about prayers for the dead is pretty straightforward and makes a lot of sense. When people die, they are either headed for heaven or hell. Even if they're on their way "up," they might have to go through the spiritual car wash known as purgatory, "the final purification of the elect"(CCC 1031).

In purgatory we feel the consequences of our sins. Remember, Christ dealt with the eternal consequences of sin — that is, death — but the temporal punishment still has to be dealt with. It's like when my kid doesn't clean her room as I've asked. I'll forgive her when she's sorry, but she's still going to have to clean (and maybe do some extra, too).

Unless you're God, you have no idea who currently resides in heaven apart from those holy people the Church has declared saints. Similarly, we don't know our own fate. Nothing is guaranteed in this life. It's not that God will ever let us down, but we'd be silly to fully trust in ourselves. He leaves us free to choose life or death (see Jos 24:15). That's why Paul says we need to work out our salvation in "fear and trembling" (Phil 2:12).

But don't forget: as members of the Body of Christ, we're all connected. We're a family. And that doesn't mean only people who are alive on this earth. Every member of your family as far back as you can trace it (and beyond) is "alive." Every human being ever conceived has an immortal soul. We all live forever, either with or without God. And our prayers for deceased members of the family are just as effective as for those chatting with us in the kitchen at Thanksgiving.

In the Second Book of Maccabees, Judas Maccabeus offered prayers and sacrifice for a bunch of his buddies who had died in a battle. He felt it his duty because, after their demise, he discovered they hadn't been faithful to God's command to stay away from idols. So, "they turned to prayer, beseeching that the sin which had been committed might be wholly blotted out" (12:42). Taking up a collection to be offered for the sin of their fallen comrades, Judas and his men "made atonement for the dead, that they might be delivered from their sin" (12:45).

Quoting St. John Chrysostom, the *Catechism* references another Old Testament story with regard to offering sacrifices and praying for the dead: "If Job's sons were purified by their father's sacrifice, why would we doubt that our offerings for the dead bring them some consolation? Let us not hesitate to help those who have died and to offer our prayers for them." Notice Chrysostom says "help" them in addition to offering prayers. That's because "the Church also commends almsgiving, indulgences, and works of penance undertaken on behalf of the dead" (CCC 1032).

Returning the Favor

Not only can we pray for souls in purgatory, but they can pray for us. St. Cyprian of Carthage exhorted,

> Let us on both sides [of death] always pray for one another. Let us relieve burdens and afflictions by mutual love, that if one of us, by the swiftness of divine condescension, shall go hence first, our love may continue in the presence of the Lord, and our prayers for our brethren and sisters not cease in the presence of the Father's mercy.[59]

I highly suggest you ask for the saints' intercession. Why? Because they are already much closer to Christ than we are. Inflamed with the love of God, they love us even more than we love them. Their prayers unleash grace through the power of divine charity. There is a difference, however, between our prayers and theirs.

Souls in purgatory can't pray for themselves because their time of merit is over. In other words, they can no longer choose to do good things, because once in purgatory they can't sin. They're on autopilot, so to speak, on their way to heaven no matter what. But they need us. Like the paralytic in the Gospel who had to be lowered through the roof to Jesus, they need our prayers for their well-being (see Mk 2:1-12). We, on the other hand, can pray for ourselves and the souls in purgatory, gaining reward because it is a good work which we still must choose to perform.

There's no doubt about it: prayer is incredibly powerful. Think of how much good you can do by interceding for both the deceased and living members of God's family. The great Benedictine Dom Hubert van Zeller said that in prayer we're using our "human powers to their highest possible limit."[60] In fact, we're surpassing that limit because we're praying through supernatural grace. Of course, the opposite is true as well. By not praying, we're throwing away the gift of conversation and union with God.

God has put his love into our hearts and desires that love be returned. We express that love through prayer. And since each of us is a unique individual, the love we give back to God is a unique expression of his love. That's why our prayers are always ultimately ordered to God. Even when we pray to the holy souls in purgatory, Mary, or any of the saints, we're praying through the grace of God and thus giving praise to him.

CHAPTER 12

Practically Speaking

In the chapter on meditation, I mentioned that Sacred Scripture is a rich source of material for prayer. It's not the only kind of spiritual reading, but it's the best. After all, it's the Word of God. Pope Benedict XVI agreed.

In his apostolic exhortation *Verbum Domini* ("The Word of God"), Pope Benedict stated, "The word of God is at the basis of all authentic Christian spirituality" (86). This is because "all scripture is inspired by God" (2 Tm 3:16). What other book can truthfully make that claim? Not a one. So let's focus a bit more on the special role of the Bible in our life of prayer.

If you've ever cracked open the missal during Mass or plopped down in your plush recliner to read the Bible, you've probably noticed it spans a long time and has many human authors. As such, it contains different writing styles and genres. There are narratives, poems, parables, prophecies, and so forth. But while many human authors wrote it over the ages, the *Catechism* tells us that God is "the principal author of Sacred Scripture" (304). That's why reading the Bible isn't like reading any other book. It's a sacred text. Therefore, "prayer should accompany the reading of sacred Scripture" (*Dei Verbum* 25). And using Scripture to pray is an ancient form of prayer called Lectio Divina.

Lectio Divina

Lectio Divina is essentially reading and praying over the Bible. Pope Benedict XVI attributes a "primordial role" in its development to Origen (third century), from whose works Sts. Ambrose and Augustine learned the method.[61] "While you attend to this Lectio Divina," says Origen, "seek aright and with unwavering faith in God the hidden sense which is present in most passages of the divine Scriptures."[62]

Because it's the story of how we're saved, the Bible is an essential part of our dialogue with God. "When you read the Bible," says St. Augustine, "God speaks to you; when you pray, you speak to God."[63] Lectio Divina is important because it leads to an "encounter with Christ, the living Word of God."[64] Far from mere reading, it's an engagement with divinity.

If you've tried it, you might have noticed it basically follows the same format as other types of meditation. But since the Bible is a divine text, Lectio Divina is in a league by itself. For this reason, it's one of the most important tools in your prayer toolbox.

There are four basic steps:

1. Reading
2. Meditation
3. Prayer
4. Contemplation

Reading Scripture is a bit trickier than reading some other types of literature. After all, it's a pretty ancient text, and unless we're familiar with the age in which it was written, it's not always clear what's going on. So the first step when reading the Bible is to determine the literal sense. The question we ask ourselves is, "What is the author of this passage trying to say?" This puts the passage in its original context and ensures we're starting from the right spot. (A solid commentary or good Bible dictionary is a necessity.)

Once we have a decent idea of what's being said, we move to meditation. At this point we're asking: What does this text say to me personally? Is there something here that catches my attention? Is the Lord speaking to me? If yes, this moves us to pray. If no, keep reading. As noted in a previous chapter, true prayer doesn't consist of method. It's the result of the method. True prayer is the movement of the heart toward God.

Lectio Divina concludes with contemplation, "during which we take up, as a gift from God," says Pope Benedict, "his own way of seeing and judging reality" (*Verbum Domini* 87). In other words, contemplating Scripture gives us the mind of Christ so we can see the world as it really is. It gives us the ability to discern the "thoughts and intentions of the heart" (Heb 4:12). This is the power of reading and praying over the Word of God.

Guigo the Carthusian, who was either a twelfth-century monk or local Italian muscle, wrote a masterpiece on Lectio Divina called *The Ladder of Monks*. (I guess that answers the question.) He summarizes the method in this manner: "Reading seeks the sweetness of the blessed life, meditation finds it, prayer asks for it, and contemplation tastes it."[65] Tastes it? Yep. True to his ethnicity, Guigo compares it to eating a fine meal. "Reading places solid food in the mouth; meditation chews and breaks it; prayer extracts the flavor; contemplation is the very sweetness that gives joy and refreshes."[66] (Anyone else getting hungry?) Guigo must have been looking at the same menu as the psalmist who proclaims, "Taste and see that the Lord is good!" (Ps 34:8).

"Read, meditate, pray, contemplate…. Hey, Matt, didn't you say contemplation isn't something we can make happen on our own?" Yes, and I commend you. Go grab a cheap, plastic, imported toy out of the prize box. Yes, contemplation is a gift from God. We can't conjure it up on our own. Likewise, Lectio Divina isn't something that you can simply whip out of your pocket and complete whenever you feel like it. Our lives are meant to be constant, living prayers. Lectio (as the cool kids call it) must be prepared for and practiced repeatedly. It's an extension of the rest of your life. Otherwise, says Guigo, the "exterior letters will not profit the reader at all."[67]

While Lectio Divina has grown in popularity over the last few years, there's an aspect about it that not many consider, but is vitally important. Because it's based on Scripture, Lectio is far more effective and fruitful when you know more about the overall story of the Bible. When you read the masters of this method like Guigo, you quickly realize that much of this kind of prayer makes connections to other parts of the Bible, the big story of our salvation. So if you don't already know the Bible relatively well, make an effort to grow in your knowledge so as to make your prayers over it richer.

Finally, as with all kinds of prayer, Lectio Divina is meant to lead to action. It's meant to transform the way we live. We don't "put on the mind of Christ" just to think differently. Lectio is meant to make us more humble, more patient, more loving — more like Christ.

Psalm Response

Praying the Scriptures is always valuable, but certain parts of the Holy Writ stand out. Among them would be Psalms, the "masterwork of prayer in the Old Testament" (CCC 2585). The psalms are so important that we hear them at every celebration of Mass. And they're not simply read. "The Psalter is the book in which the Word of God becomes man's prayer," says the *Catechism* (see 2587). In other words, we're praying the very words of God back to God. That's powerful.

Even more interesting, Jesus prayed the psalms. Think about that for a moment. God himself was praying the Word of God back to God. Whoa! I guess if the incarnate Second Person of the Trinity thinks it's important to pray the psalms, we should, too.

Psalms is an interesting book because often there are a couple of things going on at once. One the one hand, they frequently recount stories of God's great works in the history of Israel. They tell a story. But at the same time, the psalms express the reflections and musings of the human author's experience. And even though the literal events discussed in the book of Psalms are ancient history, because they are written from the heart of human experience, they are easy to apply to our daily lives. If you've spent any time reading or praying them, you've probably noticed an almost automatic tendency to become the "I" in the psalms. They're very personal.

There are few people on this earth, for example, for whom Psalm 23 doesn't resonate: "The Lord is my shepherd, I shall not want.... Even though I walk through the valley of the shadow of death, I fear no evil; for thou art with me." We've all been there, haven't we?

Psalm 51 was originally written by King David after he committed adultery with Bathsheba. Crushed with shame and sorrow he cried out: "Have mercy on me, O God, according to thy steadfast love.... Wash me thoroughly from iniquity, and cleanse me from my sin!" (vv. 1-2). The psalms were written around three thousand years ago, but tell me they don't apply to you today. Go ahead, I triple-dog dare you. If you're not already doing so, start praying the psalms. Now let's talk about something else.

Prayer on the Hour

Have you ever noticed priests, deacons, or really holy-looking laypeople carrying around small, thick books with ribbons flowing out the bottom? This book is called a breviary, and it contains the Liturgy of the Hours, the official set of the Church's daily prayers (in addition to the Mass). Sometimes referred to as the Divine Office, these prayers are daily requirements for bishops, priests, and transitional deacons (guys on their way to becoming priests). The prayers are also a huge component of monastic life.

The Liturgy of the Hours is primarily made up of psalms, hymns, and other readings from Scripture that are prayed at certain times of the day. It's a bit more detailed than I have time for here, but the Liturgy of the Hours basically consists of morning (Lauds), daytime (Terce, Sext, or None depending on the time they're prayed), evening (Vespers), and night prayers (Compline).

As with so many other aspects of the Catholic faith, the Liturgy of the Hours finds its origin in the Bible itself. In Scripture we frequently see references to certain times of the day when prayers were offered. For example, in the Acts of the Apostles we read, "Now Peter and John were going up to the temple at the hour of prayer, the ninth hour" (3:1). The ninth hour was about three in the afternoon, the time of the evening sacrifice. This marked the end of the Jewish day.

While praying at the same hour of the day, the centurion Cornelius received a vision instructing him to send men to see Peter. When they arrived, Acts tells us that Peter was praying up on the roof at "about the sixth hour" (noon) (10:9).

By praying at set times during the day, the apostles and other early Christians were continuing the tradition handed on to them by their forefathers. For example, Daniel, patron saint of all lion tamers (at least he should be), was visited by an angel in a similar manner to Cornelius while praying "at the time of the evening sacrifice" (Dn 9:21). Daniel prayed "three times a day" (Dn 6:10). In fact, that's why he got tossed into the lion's den in the first place. To this day, Jews continue to pray three times a day.

The Liturgy of the Hours establishes a rhythm of prayer set to the beat of our lives. It keeps us focused on what is most important, most essential. By setting aside certain times for prayer, we're putting the world on pause and periodically putting ourselves back in the presence of God. It's all about preserving right order in our lives. If you've never tried it, I encourage you to give the Liturgy of the Hours a "go." It can really transform your prayer life.

Reading Is Fundamental

"Once a kid starts to read, the world is an open book." Remember that line? You will if you're anywhere near my age and watched Saturday morning cartoons (eating a big bowl of Cap'n Crunch until the roof of your mouth bled). The slogan is from those "Reading Is Fundamental" commercials. They were right, of course. Reading is important for natural growth. But it's even more fundamental for spiritual growth.

Unfortunately, times have changed since that commercial first ran. Video killed the radio star, and the Internet changed the way we read. Take it from a guy who travels a lot: it's increasingly rare to see people looking at magazines on flights, much less reading books with no pictures. They're glued to gaming devices, phones, or movies on their computers.

And it's not just technology. The society around us has changed, too. The world is a far more secular place than it was one hundred, twenty-five, or even five years ago. It's a challenge to find people whom you can implicitly trust, people who share the same faith and follow the same moral compass. (The arrow should always point up.) Religion is barely talked about in groups unless it's in reference to some scandal. Perhaps worse, religious conversation often deteriorates until it is nothing more than a platform from which someone spouts his often problematic opinion. Society has drifted so far from God that as individuals we need to make a pointed effort to offset negative influences. If we don't, we'll go down faster than the Titanic. That's why spiritual reading is so important. But we have to choose wisely.

In case you haven't noticed, many things we tend to consume these days in books and magazines, and on the Internet, aren't designed to encourage reflection. We're spoon-fed garbage with sugar coating (like Fruity Pebbles). Captivating, often provocative photos and punchy headlines draw us in like mosquitoes to the blue light. "It's so beautiful ... *zzzzzzt!*"

When secular media finally decides to get "serious" — that is, newscaster with thoughtful eyes and a furrowed brow — how often is it about God? (Questioning his existence doesn't count.) We're far more likely to see a prime-time story on the alarming increase in the number of people eating french fries than those dying without the sacraments. My personal favorites are serious animal crises. "There's a polar bear adrift on an iceberg that's too small for him! Noooooooooooo! Back to you in the studio, Jim."

Even worse than serious coverage about not necessarily serious issues, we're constantly assaulted with images of transitory things: cars, jewelry, beer, whatever. If we're not careful, these temporal goods can easily distract us from eternal goods. It's vital that we continually remind ourselves of the shortness of this life, that we're just passing through on our way (Lord willing) to everlasting bliss. We must rise above the vacuous society in which we live and immerse ourselves in material that will enflame our hearts. That's the role of spiritual reading, and it's so important that some spiritual writers deem it almost as important as prayer itself.

Don't get me wrong, though, I'm not saying we want to lose touch with culture. On the contrary, we need to be aware of what's out there and what's happening. The goal is to move it back toward God, to move people back toward him. But we can't lead anybody anywhere if we're stuck in the slime and muck. So what do we do? Temper our intake of secular culture. Definitely tune out blatant immorality because it will kill your soul. And watch your intake of the rest of it, too. You can't eat sugar all the time and expect to stay healthy.

But it's not just a matter of turning off your television or shutting down the computer for a bit. Unless you're seeking some meditative silence, you've got to fill that time with something good. Otherwise you'll simply turn to other distractions. Grab some good reading and feed your soul.

While there's no set list of what you should read, I'm more than willing to make some suggestions. As indicated earlier, don't leave your Bible on the shelf. It's the only one of the books you own that is divinely inspired. And if you're going to read it, start with the Gospels. Since our aim is to be like Jesus Christ, what better way to achieve that end than to read about his life and hear what he has to say? Other "no brainer" resources are the *Catechism*, saints' books, or any of the classics from the multitude of great Catholic authors. See www.MatthewSLeonard.com for some of my favorites. Your options are quite numerous.

Good reading elevates. It can show us how to live and how to please God. It can teach us who he is. The Doors singing, "Hello, I love you, won't you tell me your name" isn't based on reality. You can't fall in love with someone you don't know. Relationship with God isn't based on fleeting feelings. It's grounded on knowledge acquired by faith and reason.

It's entirely possible that some of you are presently thinking: "I don't have to elevate myself any more, Matt. I climbed through thirteen years of Catholic school (sixth grade twice)." If that thought passed through your brain, consider this. One of the most educated and intelligent theologians in the history of the Church, Thomas Aquinas, the Angelic Doctor, was so awed by a vision he had of God and the realization of how little he knew, he called all of his writings — including his massive compilation of theology called the *Summa Theologica* — nothing but "straw."

We're never going to plumb the depths of God. But we need to maintain the habit of spiritual reading because the more we know of him, the more we'll love him. It couldn't be simpler. There's no rocket science about it, no universal criteria. Read as the Spirit moves you. If after a few minutes you've got a lot to chew on, don't go further. Spiritual reading is very closely related to mental prayer. In fact, if it's doing its job, it will drive you to your knees.

Take-Home Test

Before allowing yourself the nighttime pleasure of silent contemplation under the influence of the holy comforter — that is, going to bed — it's a good idea to have a look back at the day through what's known as an examination of conscience. It's exactly what it sounds like. When you examine your conscience you reflect on how you're doing spiritually; whether or not you're progressing in holiness. Simply scan back over the events of the day to see what you did right and what you did wrong. Then thank God for what went well, and pray for grace to correct the weak spots.

The examination of conscience sounds a lot like the examination of self we perform while standing in line for confession. ("Let's see, I lost my temper twice, gossiped, set the cat on fire.... I wish this priest would hurry up.... Nuts! Now I have to confess impatience.") It's not the same thing, though they're somewhat similar.

St. Ignatius Loyola, who made this kind of examination central to his spirituality, defines two different facets or types of examination: general and particular. The general exam is what we've already alluded to: an overall inventory of spiritual growth. The particular examination deals with specific vices we're trying to eliminate or virtues we're trying to develop.

A trick that helps make your nightly examination more pleasant is to make a resolution in the morning to overcome a particular fault with which you've been dealing. "O God, please help me not talk badly about so and so because he's so ... oops." Before your feet hit the floor make a decision to do your best in that area. Then, in the evening, you can review how well you did.

While the examination of conscience is a very important tool, it's not a substitute for regular prayer. They're both important, but the examination focuses on us, while prayer focuses on God.

CHAPTER 13

Abandonment

As we've seen over the course of this book, there is a progression to prayer and our spiritual lives in general. We aren't supposed to stay spiritual babies, or even adolescents. We're called to grow up in the faith and help others do so as well. But while we've touched on many of the ideas associated with this growth, it's hard to wrap our minds around it all and keep everything straight. Vocal, meditative, and contemplative prayer? The Purgative, Illuminative, and Unitive Ways? Grace and freedom? There are a lot of moving parts.

So I want to give you the key — the simple secret that will propel you through the stages of prayer and the spiritual life like a rocket. In addition to the "normal" things we're supposed to do — Mass as often as we can, frequent confession, deep prayer — there is a key to the spiritual life that is so simple it's almost laughable. (Drum roll, please.) The secret to getting what God has prepared for us from before all time is wrapped up in one word — abandonment.

"Abandonment? Sounds almost like something I can get arrested for, Matt." It does, doesn't it? But I'm not talking about abandoning your dog, your car, or your child. I'm talking about abandoning yourself. Abandoning yourself into the hands of the God who made you. Abandoning yourself to the God who holds your very being in existence right now. Abandoning yourself to the God who out of complete humility became one of us to suffer and die so we can have the opportunity to live in happiness forever.

Nobody loves us more than God. Which means we need to start believing him. We need to let go and let God.

It's all about trustful surrender to divine providence. This is the core of Christianity. But we need to understand abandonment correctly (so you don't get arrested).

Abandonment to God's will doesn't mean sitting back and doing nothing. It's not a spiritual chill pill. Sound reason cannot be ignored when trying to figure out what God wants us to do. Use your brain. Use your friend's brain. Use anybody's brain that can help you find the way. God gave us intelligence for a reason.

Finding God's Will

Discerning the will of God isn't a free-for-all. There are definite guidelines, starting points from which we begin our discernment. There are essentially two categories of God's will. We'll call them God's "revealed will" and his "permissive will." The first kind is clear, the second not as much.

The revealed will of God is what he's already told us he wants us to do. It's pretty straightforward. "Thou shalt," and "Thou shalt not." (They don't call them the Ten Commandments for nothing.) Of course, not even the Bible tells us everything we're supposed to do. But God didn't just give us a book. He gave us a living Church through which he guides his people. If a choice we make is not in line with the teaching of the Church, we've made the wrong choice. It's that simple. We've gone against the will of God, and we'll suffer the consequences.

The first and most obvious way to follow God's will is to stay out of mortal sin. From there we attack our venial, less serious, sins through the sacraments, prayer, and other means we've discussed in these pages. That's not the end of the revealed will of God, though. Obeying God's will also means taking care of the duties that go along with our state in life.

If you have a family, for example, they are part of God's revealed will for your life. In fact, they are your first duty.

Your family even comes before your own private prayers and devotions. If I stop bathing my small children because it's crimping my morning prayer, I'm not fulfilling my God-given obligation as a parent. I'm not properly taking care of those entrusted to me. Plus, my house would stink!

Family trumps just about everything. This doesn't mean, however, you're to neglect your private devotions, job, or even other people due to obligations to your family. The family has a prior claim, but not an exclusive claim, on our time. We have other duties and obligations that must be taken care of, too. (If I don't work, they don't eat!)

Permission Granted

God's revealed will is just one side of the coin, though. We all know there are decisions we face in life that aren't answered clearly in Church teaching or determined by our station in life. Additionally, there are many things that just plain happen to us, things over which we have no control. These fall under the category of God's permissive will. And, frankly, it confuses a lot people who wonder why bad stuff is happening. "Why would God do this to me?" They think God is punishing them for some reason when they didn't even do anything wrong — that they can remember, anyway. To understand this a little better, we have to go back to our previous discussion of grace and providence from Chapter 5.

Remember, we said everything that happens is ultimately God's will because nothing can happen without God's power? He holds everything in existence, and no one can act without him. That means that, except for our sinful actions, everything that happens to us is part of God's permissive will. He permits it to happen. Even the consequences of our sins (not the sin itself) are willed by God, who sees them as opportunities to further his divine plan for our life. "Matt," you're thinking, "that sounds a bit harsh, doesn't it? Why would he do that?" Because he knows how to write straight with crooked lines.

Don't misunderstand. It's not God's plan, for example, that someone hurts you through sinful action. But he may let it happen because he knows how to bring good out of it. "We know that in everything God works for good with those who love him" (Rom 8:28).

Truth be told, often he allows misfortune in order to purify us, to get our "self" out of the picture. Too much self leaves too little room for God. Father Walter Ciszek, a Jesuit missionary to Russia in the middle of the twentieth century, was imprisoned by the Soviets for twenty-three years. Intolerable conditions, solitary confinement, torture, psychological degradation, hard labor — his ordeal was horrific.

What I found fascinating about his story was the progression of his prayer life and general relationship with God during this tribulation. For years after it all began, he describes his attitude as one of independence. He thanked God for the attributes he had received which would help him to endure hardship and perhaps even convert his captors. His focus was on others, figuring they were the only ones who needed change. This lasted for years. But things got progressively worse, and after intense suffering he finally succumbed to repeated attempts by the Soviets to procure his signed confession for crimes he didn't commit. Crushed and ashamed, he eventually began to realize he had tried to do too much on his own — and failed. He wasn't really praying for God's will to be done, just for what he thought God's will should be. What follows is the moving account of a broken man who learns complete reliance on God, regardless of his unjust circumstances:

> He was asking of me an act of total trust, allowing for no interference or restless striving on my part, no reservations, no exceptions, no areas where I could set

conditions or seem to hesitate.… Once understood, it seemed so simple. I was amazed it had taken me so long in terms of time and of suffering to learn this truth.[68]

God transformed Father Ciszek's life through the terribly sinful actions of others. After so many years of serving Our Lord, this awful series of events in his life led to what he unashamedly calls a new "conversion experience … a death and resurrection."[69]

As powerfully as he works through bad circumstances, not everything in God's permissive will has to do with negative things. Lots of things he allows are really great. He's our Father who loves to shower us with gifts and see us happy. As Jesus said: "If you then, who are evil, know how to give good gifts to your children, how much more will your Father who is in heaven give good things to those who ask him!" (Mt 7:11).

Lemonade Out of Lemons

Abandonment to divine providence is more than simply accepting what comes our way. True abandonment sees right through every situation to the holy hand of God, sure that he's guiding us to glory. It recognizes providence in every joy, sickness, or disappointment and embraces it. It's actively living what we pray in the Our Father — "Thy will be done on earth as it is in heaven."

This doesn't mean we embrace calamity, illness, or other foul situations without any further action. Embracing God's will doesn't mean we fail to work for the improvement of our circumstances. It may be God's will that you're sick, but that doesn't mean you should refuse to take your medicine. Again, use your brain. In so doing we're actually living the will of God, using the gifts he gave us.

We have a natural aversion to suffering, so embracing it can be tough. I realize that. I often have a hard time not complaining about even trivial things. But there's no room for whining once we realize God must have allowed, for example, that rainy day on our family vacation. (Though it's hard not to whine when Disney World charges a small fortune for a plastic garbage bag they label "rain poncho" just because there's a hole in the middle and a picture of a mouse on the front.) Why shouldn't we complain? Because God must have allowed that rain for a reason. Maybe a local farmer was desperate for rain. Maybe some soccer mom just couldn't handle driving to yet another practice that day. Maybe he wanted to give me an opportunity for growth — to not complain. Who knows? God does.

Regardless of the situation, as bad as it might appear, God is working. Yes, he wants us to be happy in the here and now, but his overarching concern is for our eternal salvation. We can't see all the parts in motion like he does. Embrace what happens even if you don't like it on a natural level. (Though lots of times you will.) Like any good parent, God's far more interested in preparing us for the future. He always has our eternal destination in mind. He knows what he's doing.

How many times have you told someone, "Trust me" when they questioned you? That's what God is saying to us at every moment: "Trust me. I gave you your very breath and love you more than you can possibly fathom. Trust me. I sent my only Son to die so you could live. Trust me. I want you to have inconceivable bliss and ecstasy with me forever. Trust me!" Abandonment to divine providence leads us to live as true children, completely trusting the goodness of the Father. It's the only way to find true peace and interior joy.

We are on a lifetime journey to God. And there is nothing in this passing world worth a detour. Get on the path to God and don't get off. Life is too short to take the long route because you may never get where you need to be. When someone asked St. John Vianney how best to get to God, he replied, "Quite straight, like a cannonball."

So fire away, because our union with God doesn't happen later. It starts right now. Remember, the goal is to "get in touch with Jesus as early as possible in the spiritual life, in each of its exercises, especially that of prayer, and to keep in touch with Him by all possible means and at all costs."[70]

This deep relationship with God is what we were made for. It's the only thing that will ever satisfy you. So pray for wisdom. Pray for grace. Pray to live. Why? Because prayer works!

Notes

1 Pope Benedict XVI, *Prayer* (Huntington, IN: Our Sunday Visitor, 2013), 16.

2 Benedict Baur, *In Silence with God* (New York: Scepter Publishers, 1997), 136.

3 Ibid.

4 Eugene Boylan, *Difficulties in Mental Prayer* (Notre Dame, IN: Christian Classics, 2010), 27.

5 Pope John Paul II, *Puebla: A Pilgrimage of Faith* (Boston: Daughters of St. Paul, 1979), 86.

6 Benedict Baur, *In Silence with God,* (New York: Scepter Publishers, 1997), 142.

7 Teresa of Ávila, *The Interior Castle*, trans. E. Allison Peers, (New York: Image, 2004), 5.

8 Ibid., x.

9 Ibid., 11.

10 Kieran Kavanaugh, *The Collected Works of St. John of the Cross*, trans. Otilio Rodriguez (Washington, D.C.: ICS Publications, 1991), 355.

11 The dark night of the soul actually applies to both the purification of the senses (which happens in between the Purgative and illuminative Ways) and the purification of the spirit (soul), which is the transition from the Illuminative to the Unitive Way. The title is most closely associated with this latter movement. (See *The Collected Works of St. John of the Cross*, 354).

12 Kieran Kavanaugh, *The Collected Works of St. John of the Cross*, trans. Otilio Rodriguez (Washington, D.C.: ICS Publications, 1991), 359.

13 Ibid., 403.

14 Kieran Kavanaugh, *The Collected Works of St. John of the Cross*, trans. Otilio Rodriguez (Washington, D.C.: ICS Publications, 1991), 404.

15 Reginald Garrigou-Lagrange, *Christian Perfection and Contemplation* (Rockford, IL: TAN Books and Publishers, 2003), 83.

16 Ibid., 91.

17 Edward Leen, *Progress Through Mental Prayer* (New York: Sheed & Ward, 1947), 39.

18 Ibid.

19 Joseph Ratzinger, *Behold the Pierced One* (San Francisco: Ignatius Press, 1986), 15.

20 William McDonough, *The Divine Family: The Trinity and Our Life in God* (Cincinnati: Servant, 2005), 38.

21 Scott Hahn, *Understanding "Our Father": Biblical Reflections on the Lord's Prayer* (Steubenville: Emmaus Road, 2002), 10.

22 Blessed Columba Marmion, *Christ, The Life of the Soul*, trans. Alan Bancroft (Bethesda, MD: Zaccheus Press), 6.

23 Hubert Van Zeller, *Prayer In Other Words* (Springfield, IL: Templegate, 1963), 46.

24 Scott Hahn and Mike Aquilina, *Living the Mysteries* (Huntington, IN: Our Sunday Visitor, 2003), 161.

25 Dom Jean-Baptiste Chautard, *Soul of the Apostolate* (Garden City, NY: Image, 1961), 91.

26 Alphonsus Liguori, *Prayer: The Great Means of Salvation and of Perfection,* www.basilica.org, Part III: Mental Prayer, under the section "It Disposes the Heart to the Practice of Virtues."

27 Adolphe Tanquerey, *The Spiritual Life: A Treatise on Ascetical and Mystical Theology* (Charlotte, NC: TAN Books, 2000), 323.

28 Edward Leen, *Progress Through Mental Prayer* (New York: Sheed & Ward, 1947), 158.

29 Reginald Garrigou-Lagrange, *The Three Ages of the Interior Life: Prelude of Eternal Life* (Rockford, IL: TAN Books and Publishers, 1989), 448.

30 Irenaeus of Lyons, *Against Heresies* 3.3.2.

31 Josef Pieper, *Happiness and Contemplation* (South Bend, IN: St. Augustine's Press, 1979), 71.

32 Kieran Kavanaugh, *The Collected Works of St. John of the Cross*, trans. Otilio Rodriguez (Washington, D.C.: ICS Publications, 1991), 382.

33 Ibid., 193.

34 Thomas Dubay, *Fire Within* (San Francisco: Ignatius Press, 1989), 58.

35 Different spiritual authors use different terms to describe the levels of prayer which we have generally labeled vocal, meditative, and contemplative. What some call the higher levels of meditation (e.g., prayer of simplicity) others call infused contemplation, which derives its meaning from the Latin word "*infusum,*" which means "to pour in" or "that which is poured in." In other words, it comes solely from God. Father Garrigou-Lagrange and others insist this level of prayer of infused contemplation is something to which all are called. But even within infused contemplation there are various degrees which only some may attain. St. Teresa describes the higher levels of mystical union with God that go beyond the initial stages of infused contemplation. In *The Interior Castle* and elsewhere she identifies four different degrees of mystical union, calling them the Prayer of Quiet, the Prayer of Union, Spiritual Betrothal (or Conforming Union), and Spiritual Marriage (Transforming Union).

36 Thomas Dubay, *Fire Within* (San Francisco: Ignatius Press, 1989), 24.

37 Ibid., 23.

38 Ibid.

39 Edward Leen, *Progress Through Mental Prayer* (New York: Sheed & Ward, 1947), 123.

40 Ibid., 127.

41 Mary Fabyan Windeatt, *Saint Margaret Mary and the Promises of the Sacred Heart of Jesus* (Rockford, IL: TAN Books and Publishers, 1953), 44.

42 Edward Leen, *Progress Through Mental Prayer* (New York: Sheed & Ward, 1947), 138.

43 Max Picard, *The World of Silence* (Chicago: Gateway, 1964), 3.

44 Ibid., 7.

45 Ibid., 1.

46 Kieran Kavanaugh, *The Collected Works of St. John of the Cross*, trans. Otilio Rodriguez (Washington, D.C.: ICS Publications, 1991), 92.

47 Edward Leen, *Progress Through Mental Prayer* (New York: Sheed & Ward, 1947), 274.

48 Kieran Kavanaugh, *The Collected Works of St. John of the Cross*, trans. Otilio Rodriguez (Washington, D.C.: ICS Publications, 1991), 95.

49 Edward Leen, *Progress Through Mental Prayer* (New York: Sheed & Ward, 1947), 275.

50 *The Observer*, May 17, 2008.

51 Olivier Clement, *The Roots of Christian Mysticism* (New York: New City Press, 1996), 153-154.

52 Benedict Baur, *In Silence with God* (New York: Scepter Publishers, 1997), 115.

53 Olivier Clement, *The Roots of Christian Mysticism* (New York: New City Press, 1996), 154.

54 Teresa of Ávila, *The Interior Castle* (New York: Image, 1961), 66.

55 Karol Wojtyla, *Love and Responsibility*, trans. H.T. Willetts, (San Francisco: Ignatius, 1993), 98.

56 Kieran Kavanaugh, *The Collected Works of St. John of the Cross*, trans. Otilio Rodriguez (Washington, D.C.: ICS Publications, 1991), 124.

57 Louis de Montfort, *True Devotion to Mary* (Rockford, IL: TAN Books & Publishers, 1985), 18.

58 Dom Jean-Baptiste Chautard, *The Soul of the Apostolate* (Charlotte, NC: TAN Books, 2012), 289.

59 Cyprian of Carthage, Epistle 56[60]:5.

60 Hubert van Zeller, *Prayer in Other Words* (Springfield, IL: Templegate, 1963), 15.

61 Benedict XVI, *The Fathers* (Huntington, IN: Our Sunday Visitor, 2008), 42.

62 Ibid., 41.

63 *Verbum Domini*, 86. *Enarrationes in Psalmos*, 85, 7: PL 37, 1086.

64 Ibid., 87. Final Message, III, 9.

65 Scott Hahn, ed. *Letter & Spirit The Authority of Mystery: The Word of God and the People of God* (Steubenville, OH: St. Paul Center for Biblical Theology, 2006), 176.

66 Ibid.

67 Ibid., 181.

68 Walter Ciszek S.J., *He Leadeth Me* (San Francisco: Ignatius Press, 1973), 77.

69 Ibid., 78.

70 Eugene Boylan, *Difficulties in Mental Prayer* (Notre Dame, IN: Christian Classics, 2010), 27.

CPSIA information can be obtained
at www.ICGtesting.com
Printed in the USA
JSHW080351051122
32626JS00003B/10